John G. Reid

SIX-

crucial

DECADES

Times of Change in the History of the Maritimes

NIMBUS PUBLISHING LIMITED

Published by:
Nimbus Publishing Limited
P.O. Box 9301, Station A
Halifax, N.S. B3K 5N5

Design: Kathy Kaulbach

Typesetting: A.J. Copyrite

Printing and Binding:
Sentinel Printing Limited , N.S.

Canadian Cataloguing in Publication Data

Reid, John G. (John Graham), 1948-
  Six crucial decades

Bibliography: p.
Includes index.
ISBN 0-920852-84-X

1. Maritimes Provinces - History. I. Title.

FC2028.R44 1987   971   C87-093920-3
F1035.8.R45 1987

Printed and bound in Canada

CONTENTS

for Jackie

PREFACE

This book originated as a series of public lectures given at Saint Mary's University in the winter of 1986. It makes no claim to be a comprehensive history of the Maritime provinces. What it does offer is a series of interpretive treatments of important phases in the Maritimes' historical development. Each of these six crucial decades was a time of change. Each of the decades, through the events that took place and through the coming together of larger historical forces, altered the course of the region's history. Had matters turned out differently in any one of them, life in today's Maritime provinces — if the provinces existed at all — would not have been as we know it.

In writing about these six decades, I have aimed at synthesizing existing knowledge rather than providing a work of original research scholarship. Although I have used my own research in some passages, and although of course I take full responsibility for the conclusions reached, I have drawn heavily on the work of other historians. To do so in the field of Maritime history is a rewarding task, because so much fine scholarship has emerged in the last twenty or so years. Up until the late 1960s, despite the achievements of a few outstanding historians, the study of the Maritime provinces was not well established as a branch of history. Fortunately, that situation has now changed. The establishment of the regional journal *Acadiensis* in Fredericton in 1971, under the editorship of Phillip Buckner, was especially important in stimulating the interest of scholars, and in 1987 both *Acadiensis* and the field as a whole continue to flourish. In this book, intended primarily for the non-specialist reader, I have kept footnote citations to a minimum. However, those who wish to explore in greater detail will find suggestions in the "further reading" sections of the chapters.

A few words should be said about use of the word "region." I have not hesitated to refer to the Maritime provinces, or to the territory that we now know as such, as a region. By doing this, I do not mean that the Maritimes should be regarded as uniform. Historically, just as today, there have been strong elements of internal diversity, conflict, disparity; and yet there are good historical reasons for treating this territory as a whole. Originally comprehending the lands of the culturally-related Micmac and Maliseet-Passamaquoddy native peoples, the area came in the seventeenth century to form the major part of the French colony of Acadia. For a time in the eighteenth century, the British colony of Nova Scotia covered it entirely, until the colonies of Prince Edward Island and New Brunswick (as well as the shorter-lived colony of Cape Breton) were split off. In the first half of the nineteenth century the three jurisdictions were often collectively described as the Lower Provinces, while the term 'Maritime Provinces' appeared frequently in the Confederation debates of the 1860s and entered into everyday usage in the early part of the present century. For centuries, therefore, diversity has been accompanied by a perceived general identity.

Nevertheless, within the regional framework, this book does emphasize the importance of complexity and conflict. Recent historical writing on the Maritimes leaves no room for comfortable stereotypes, and the reality is that the history of the region is shot through with struggles between people divided by nationality, ethnicity, economic interest, and social class. Sometimes those struggles were resolved peacefully, while at other times they brought disaster for large groups of the region's inhabitants. Maritime history — the real Maritime history — defies any attempt to make the past sound quaint or heroic, unless it is the heroism of ordinary people coping with threats to their lives and livelihoods. Often dramatic, not always pleasant to recount or contemplate, the major historical events and processes have shaped the region as it is today. Not all of them can be considered in a book as short as this one. What does emerge from the study of these six decades, I believe, is that historians have come to grips with the region's past more fully now than ever before.

The writing of a book sometimes seems to be a lonely task, and yet it is one that cannot be fulfilled without the help of others. I especially thank my colleague Colin Howell, who encouraged me to present the series of lectures on which this work is based, read the full manuscript, and generally gave valued support throughout. The lecture series was a project of the Division of Continuing Education at Saint Mary's University and of the Gorsebrook Research Institute, and I thank Jim Sharpe and John Chamard for this sponsorship. I am grateful also to those who attended, and especially to the half-dozen or so who regularly gathered afterwards for refreshment and continued discussion.

Week by week, the lectures were discussed in radio interviews on C.B.C's "Radio Noon," and I thank Patrick Napier and Elizabeth Haines for their stimulating questions, as well as Sue Dexter for initiating the interview series.

Portions of the manuscript were read by colleagues at Saint Mary's and elsewhere, and I am grateful to David Frank, Harold McGee, Ian McKay, Neil MacKinnon, Barry Moody, and Peter Toner for their valuable comments. I also much appreciate the advice I received on more specific points from Gene Barrett, Steve Davis, and Raymond Léger. None of them, of course, is responsible for my remaining errors.

The manuscript was typed and retyped by Lane Thomas, whose skill with the word processor was matched by a consistent good humour that was much more than my untidy script deserved. Elizabeth Eve's editorial work brought about many stylistic improvements, and Peter Kidd provided editorial guidance in the later stages; they and Dorothy Cooper, managing editor of Nimbus Publishing, were instrumental in bringing the book to publication.

My wife and daughter have contributed in innumerable ways, and the chapters that follow are written for them both. The book itself belongs to Jackie, while the past experiences it describes are part of the legacy that eventually will be passed on to Jane's generation of Maritimers.

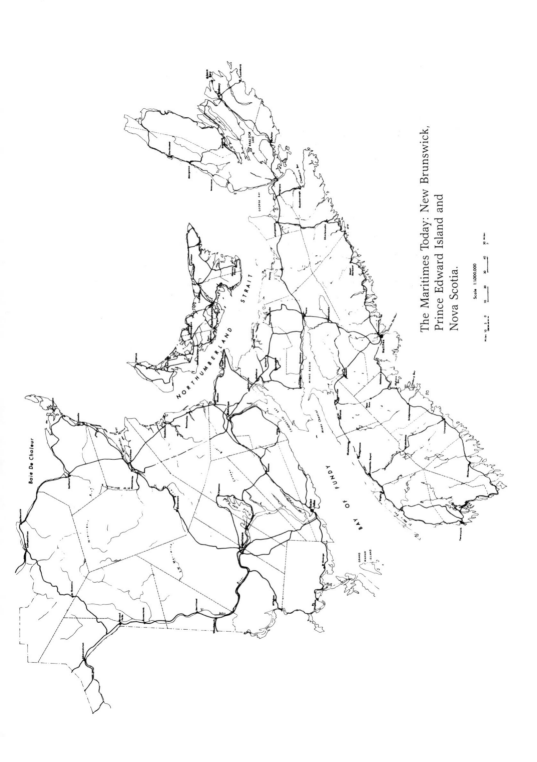

The Maritimes Today: New Brunswick, Prince Edward Island and Nova Scotia.

Scale 1:1,000,000

THE 1600s:

DECADE OF COLONIZATION

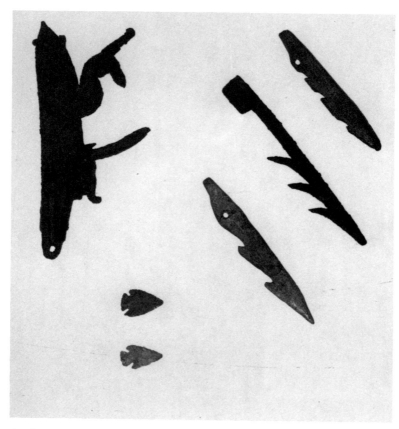

Artifacts from the Contact period, Micmac and European.

During the decade from 1600 to 1610, the Maritime provinces of Canada had not yet been invented. Had events turned out differently in this decade, they might never have been invented, and undoubtedly the entire course of the history of the region would have been altered. Already by the year 1600, the human history of the territory now comprising the Maritime provinces was in an era of rapid change. People had been living there continuously for more than 10,000 years and the direct ancestors of the Micmac and Maliseet-Passamaquoddy Indian peoples had been established since about 1000 B.C.[1] Since then their culture had altered and evolved. Among the periods of most significant change was the century following the first European contacts in or about the year 1500.[2]

The visits of European explorers and fishermen did not lead immediately to any permanent European presence, and yet they left their mark on native culture. By trading furs, the Indian peoples acquired European artifacts such as metal knives and copper kettles, which could be used to make hunting and domestic tasks easier. The purpose of the trade, for them, was not to change radically their existing way of life but rather to strengthen it.

Trade, however, brought more to native people than the artifacts they wanted. It also brought European disease. Never before exposed to diseases such as smallpox and influenza, Indian people had little or no immunity. Together with changes in diet caused by eating dried European foods acquired in trade, and in some cases problems of alcoholism, disease brought about massive changes in the size of the Indian population. In 1600 the Micmac people probably numbered about 3,500. A hundred years before, they may have been as many as 35,000.[3]

The depletion of native population before 1600 was a human tragedy on a scale that later generations can only guess at. A few years after, an old Micmac chief told a French priest that in his youth he had seen his people "as thickly planted . . . as the hairs on his head". Now, the priest reported back to France, the Micmac "are astonished and often complain that, since the French mingle with and carry on trade with them, they are dying fast, and the population is thinning out".[4]

There were also other changes. The fur trade caused Indian peoples to change the yearly cycle of their lives. Instead of harvesting diverse food resources — river and coastal fisheries, inland hunting grounds, and gathering of nuts and berries were among the most important — in long-established patterns that varied from place to place, native bands now increasingly centered their attention on the summer trade with European ships. Inland bands would spend more time at the coast, and there was a tendency for the time and energy devoted to hunting beaver to detract from more traditional pursuits. Disruption of food supplies, and eventual dependence on European trade goods, were among the subtle and far-reaching effects of European contact on native society and culture. In the long term the opportunity for trading profits would also tend to make native society less coherent, as individuals asserted their claims to own fur-trapping lands, as opposed to the more traditional collective ownership.[5]

Yet it would be entirely wrong to think of the Micmac and Maliseet in 1600 as societies falling apart. They were societies in the grip of massive changes that had already had tragic consequences for many individuals and families. They were societies under strain. The decade of the 1600s would show that they were societies which had not broken under that strain. The native peoples of the region still retained a resilience that showed in their response to the onset of European colonization.

The story of the early French colonization of Acadia has often been told, and needs only brief outlining here. The colony of Acadia was formally created in 1603, when King Henry IV of France granted a charter to Pierre Du Gua, Sieur de Monts, to authorize de Monts to settle and govern Acadia. De Monts was also granted a ten-year monopoly of the fur trade in the colony. In return for these grants, he undertook to send at least 60 settlers to Acadia each year, and to sponsor efforts to convert native people to Christianity.[6]

The Sieur de Monts was a former military officer who had already had experience in North America. His first visit to the

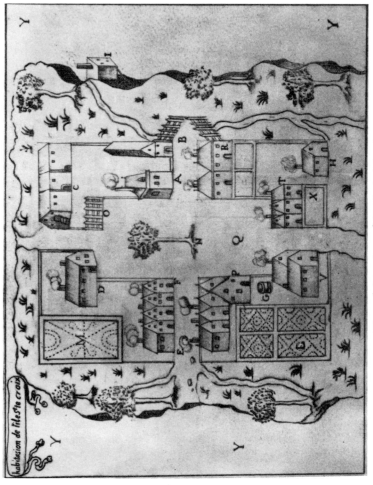

Champlain's view of St. Croix Island

hemisphere had probably been in the year 1600 when he was one of the participants in an unsuccessful French colonizing attempt at Tadoussac, on the St. Lawrence River. The boundaries of Acadia, as defined in 1603, indicated a more southerly area of interest. Extending from the 40th to the 46th line of latitude, the colony included the entire eastern seaboard from present-day New Jersey to Cape Breton Island.

In March 1604, de Monts set sail from the French port of Le Havre. His fleet of three ships carried some 80 colonists who would spend the following winter in Acadia. Of most of them, no exact record has survived. It may be that some were criminals and vagrants who had been conscripted for the venture. Among the few whose names and biographies are known was Samuel de Champlain, a writer and cartographer who had made a voyage up the St. Lawrence River the previous summer. Champlain carried no official title in 1604, but took charge of the process of finding a site for colonization, and emerged as one of the leaders of the colony.

Champlain's choice of the first settlement site proved disastrously mistaken. St. Croix Island (later known as Dochet's Island) was located in the St. Croix River, half a mile from shore and not far from present-day St. Andrews, New Brunswick. It was a tiny island, and its chief attraction was strategic: no enemy ship could pass it without coming within cannon-range. It also had some disadvantages, in that there was no fresh water supply and, after trees had been cut down to build housing for the colonists, no source of firewood either. For these necessities, and for hunting, the settlers would have to make the crossing to the river bank. In summer, that was merely inconvenient; in winter, it was difficult and dangerous.

To be fair, Champlain and his colleagues were understandably ill-informed about the Acadian climate. Prevailing European geographical theories held that climate was determined solely by north-south latitude. By that standard Acadia should have had weather very similar to that of the south of France. The influence of the continental land mass of North America, and of ocean currents, ensured in fact that this was not so.[7] "There are six months of winter in this country," Champlain tersely observed in a later account of the episode.[8]

The results for the colonists were devastating. At least 35 of the 80 died of scurvy, caused by lack of fresh fruit and vegetables, and only ten were unaffected by the disease. The winter was exceptionally severe that year, with the first snow falling in early

Champlain's map, 1612

October. Confined on their island, residents of the small "habitation" lived on salt meat, and melted snow for water. Only in March 1605 did they successfully establish contact with Passamaquoddy Indian people and trade with them for additional food supplies.[9]

In the spring de Monts and Champlain began to look in earnest for a site further south. They searched in vain. Despite coasting down as far as the Cape Cod peninsula, the small expedition could not identify any location that had the required combination of a good harbour, potentially fertile land, and cooperative native people. Ironically, the rejected territories would soon support the populous New England colonies that would play a leading role in the later British conquest of Acadia.

As it was, de Monts had to make a difficult decision. What alternative could be found to the unsuccessful St. Croix site? As a temporary measure, until further explorations could be made, the choice was made to move across the Bay of Fundy to a location first visited by the colonizing fleet in June 1604: Port Royal, near today's Annapolis Royal, Nova Scotia. Port Royal had the advantage of offering a mainland location on a safe harbour. Also important was the receptive attitude of the local Micmac band, headed by its chief, Membertou. Reputedly over 100 years old, Membertou was a strong leader who also had the powers of a shaman, or medicine-man. For the remainder of his life — he died in 1611 — he was a consistent supporter of the French presence at Port Royal.[10]

Membertou established a close personal friendship with one of de Monts' senior lieutenants, Jean de Biencourt de Poutrincourt. Poutrincourt, a nobleman and military officer, had been impressed by the scenic beauty of Port Royal, and in the summer of 1604 de Monts had promised him a land grant in the area.[11] The grant was confirmed by Henry IV in early 1606, and so when Poutrincourt returned to Acadia later that year after spending the winter in France, he had a new personal stake in the colony.[12]

By 1606, the French colony of Acadia was in better condition than it had been during the previous two years. The winter of 1605-06 had been relatively mild, and only a few colonists had died of scurvy. Among them, ironically, were the Catholic priest and the Protestant minister. This early colonizing effort, unlike later ones in Acadia, included both Catholic and Protestant participants. Tradition holds, probably correctly, that the two clergymen were buried in the same grave: "to see," in a contemporary's sardonic phrase, "whether they could rest in peace together in death, since they were unable to reach agreement in life."[13]

The winter of 1606-07 was the most successful yet enjoyed by the colonists in Acadia. There were no food shortages, and although scurvy was not eliminated entirely, the French writer Marc Lescarbot recorded that only four deaths had resulted.[14] Lescarbot, a friend of Poutrincourt, spent the winter in the colony and in a later *History of New France* he presented a favourable picture of what his friend had achieved in Acadia. Champlain recalled similarly that "we passed this winter very pleasantly, and had good fare . . . "[15] It was during this time that Lescarbot's famous *Theatre of Neptune* was first produced, and also founded was Champlain's "Order of Good Cheer," an informal dining club in which the colonists took their turn in hunting to provide food for the table.

The good cheer did not last long. Between 1604 and 1607, the price of beaver furs rose in France by 150 percent.[16] Superficially, that seemed to be a healthy trend for the Acadian colonists, who could sell their furs at a good profit. In reality, two serious dangers were arising. One was that there would be competition from rival merchants who would take advantage of the many secluded harbours on the Acadian coastline to land a crew and trade illegally for furs, thus breaking into the monopoly of de Monts. There had always been such competition, but rising prices would inevitably intensify the problem. Secondly, there were merchants who, for similar reasons, were actively pressing the French government to revoke the monopoly altogether and declare free access to the furs of the region.

De Monts took this latter danger seriously. He could hardly do otherwise, as the Duc de Sully, chief minister of Henry IV, was known to believe that attempts at colonization of the northern parts of North America were unlikely to prove successful, and that the fur trade monopoly in Acadia was a useless restriction. De Monts had returned to France in the fall of 1605 to counter the threat. In the spring of 1607 he sent word to Port Royal that he had been unsuccessful, and that the monopoly had been cancelled. Confronted by large losses, arising from the expenses of colonization, de Monts instructed Poutrincourt, Champlain, and the other colonists to abandon Port Royal and return to France.[17]

The first major French colonizing effort in Acadia had thus ended in failure. High hopes of finding precious metals, of conquering great native empires, or of finding a sea passage to the lucrative trading markets of Asia, had quickly proved unrealistic. Even the more modest idea of basing colonization on fur-trading profits had also proved unworkable. De Monts was not yet finished with North America, but from 1608 his efforts (and those of Champlain) were focused on the potentially more productive fur-trading territories of the St. Lawrence Valley. One individual who was not disillusioned with Acadia was Poutrincourt. For the moment, though, he lacked the financial support that would be needed if the colony were to be re-established.

From all appearances, it must have seemed that French colonization in Acadia was a dead issue in 1607, and yet the significance of this series of events can only be fully assessed when put in a European context. Just why did this first French effort in Acadia take place in the decade of the 1600s rather than sooner or later? Was the timing coincidental? The answer is that coincidence had little or nothing to do with it. Strong economic and political forces were at work in Europe, reaching a peak in this decade. It was already a hundred years since European fishermen and explorers had made contact with the coast of today's Maritime provinces. Norse voyagers may in fact have landed some five centuries before that — certainly they were in Newfoundland. The Norse presence in North America was fleeting, however, and European contact was re-established within a few years before or after the year 1500.

As to exactly who was the first European of that era to set foot in the Maritime region, we do not know. It may have been the explorer John Cabot in 1497, or the later explorer Gaspar Corte-Real in 1501. More likely it was a fisherman whose name has never appeared on any written record. What is clear is that fishing vessels of various European nationalities — French, English, Spanish, Portuguese, Basque — continued to visit these coasts. They came to take on fresh water, to build temporary stages for drying fish, to do some fur-trading on the side. They might stay for a few hours, or for a summer fishing season, but never year-round. Only in the 1600s was this pattern conclusively changed in the region. A forerunner of the change was an ill-fated attempt by another would-be colonial promoter, the Marquis de la Roche, to found a colony on Sable Island in 1598. Forty convicts and about ten armed guards lived there for five years before the venture collapsed in violent conflict.[18] It would be left to the de Monts expedition to make the real beginning of French settlement.

Why, then, was the pattern of a hundred years broken in the 1600s? One reason was economic. The demand for North American furs, and especially beaver furs, developed on a large scale in Europe only in the latter part of the previous century.

Small shipments of furs brought back by fishermen had stimulated the demand and led to the emergence of the beaver-fur hat as a major fashion item for men. This had two implications for North American colonization: first, that it provided a possible source of revenue to fund the high costs of founding colonies, and secondly, that (unlike the fisheries) the fur trade required extended contacts with native peoples and thus there was more incentive to make year-round settlements.[19]

There was also a political reason for the colonization of the 1600s. Spain and Portugal had long been colonial powers in central and South America. Their empires had quickly aroused the admiration of other European nations, which looked enviously at the gold and silver drawn especially from New Spain, and at the feats of conquest by which large native empires had been destroyed. The nations of northern Europe had made some efforts to follow the Spanish example, but never with any success. The disastrous attempt by Jacques Cartier and the Sieur de Roberval from 1541 to 1543 to establish a French colony, near the present site of Quebec City, was one example.[20] After that time, France became preoccupied with internal political disputes, until in the 1590s the country emerged from the series of civil wars known as the Wars of Religion. Only then was the government of France able to turn its attention once again to the Americas as a possible source of wealth, power and prestige.

When de Monts was granted his charter in 1603, his merchant investors hoped the colony of Acadia would be a productive investment of capital in the new and flourishing fur trade. From the point of view of the royal government, the colony was to be a start in the process of developing an overseas empire to rival those of Spain and Portugal. De Monts, like other European colonial promoters of the time, was faced with the difficult task of trying to satisfy both of these aspirations at the same time. The task was made more difficult by other complications. For one thing, merchant communities were divided by competitive rivalries. This was true even within particular port towns, such as La Rochelle or St. Malo, where de Monts obtained much of his capital. The result was seen in the damaging attacks on his monopoly that de Monts encountered from the start. Furthermore, the royal government was not unanimously convinced of the merits of colonization. Although Henry IV himself was sympathetic, his chief minister Sully was sceptical. To be a colonial promoter in these circumstances was no easy task.

Thus, although there were strong, long-term economic and

political forces operating to favour colonization in the 1600s, there were also practical difficulties that stood in the way. Add to these the difficulties of adaptation to the North American environment that would face the colonists on arrival, and the failure of the Acadian colony in 1607 becomes readily understandable. It becomes even more explicable in the context that the experience of the de Monts colony was not just a French experience, but a northern European one.

France was not the only country to feel the effects of long-term forces leading towards North American colonization. The possible profits to be made from fur-trading were obvious to others, such as English and Dutch merchants. Both England and the Netherlands were emerging in the decade of the 1600s from a long period of political and military preoccupation with European affairs. Both had been at war with Spain for several decades. England concluded its peace treaty with Spain in 1604, while the Dutch republic signed a 12-year truce with Spain in 1609.

From those countries too came an outflow of economic and political energy into colonization in the decade of the 1600s. England had already made its claim to ownership of Newfoundland, and now in 1606 it proclaimed the existence of two other North American colonies: North and South Virginia. South Virginia was to be a southern colony, centred in the area still known as Virginia. North Virginia was defined as extending from the 38th to the 45th lines of latitude, and thus went far enough northwards to include a major part of the Nova Scotian peninsula. To complicate matters further, the Netherlands would act just a few years later, in 1614, to claim the territory from the 40th to the 45th parallels for its New Netherlands Company.[21]

In the decade of the 1600s, however, France and England were the two northern European nations most active in North American colonization. Potentially, their interests were in conflict. In practical terms, each was able to found colonies only on a limited basis. The English colonies in this decade included the South Virginia settlement at Jamestown, and its North Virginia equivalent at Sagadahoc, in present-day Maine. Both were founded in 1607, and three years later came the settlement of John Guy at Cupids Cove, in Newfoundland.

All of these colonies proved fragile. The Jamestown settlement survived, but only narrowly. Up until 1612, when the Virginia Company began successfully to develop a tobacco-based economy, the tiny colony struggled to cope with food shortages, internal disputes, and conflicts with native peoples. The Cupids settlement suffered from some of the same problems. It too survived, but only after disputes between Guy and the English-based Newfoundland Company had seriously threatened its existence in 1614. The Sagadahoc venture failed entirely. A severe winter in 1607-08, disputes with Abenaki Indian people, and the failure to find mines of gold and silver — "the mayne intended benefit" of the colony, wrote one discouraged participant — all combined to bring about the abandonment of the settlement in the fall of 1608.[22]

When the de Monts colony in Acadia is examined in a comparative context, therefore, two major points become clear. First, that the enterprise of de Monts was no isolated event. It proceeded from the same economic and political forces that were stimulating other northern European colonial attempts in this decade. Secondly, that despite these strong forces, such ventures could easily result in failure. Problems in adjusting to the climate and environment, and financial problems arising from the difficulties encountered in trying to develop an economic base, were common to all North American colonial ventures at the time. So too was the crucial importance of developing a close relationship with native people. For the early colonizers reaching North America was in many cases just the beginning of their troubles, as they quickly discovered the difficulties of settlement.

The evacuation of Port Royal by the French colonists in 1607 could reasonably have been expected to mark the end of French efforts at colonization in this part of North America. Just as the Sagadahoc failure a year later was described by its chief promoter as "a wonderful discouragement" to future English colonial schemes, so the abandonment of Port Royal could only confirm the cynicism of de Monts' critics.[23] Furthermore, when de Monts and Champlain turned their attention in 1608 to the St. Lawrence Valley, it seemed clear that Acadia was to be by-passed from now on. Had this turned out in fact to be true, it is hard to estimate what the consequences would have been. Would Acadia (under some other name) have been colonized by another European nationality, such as English, Dutch, or Scots? Would Acadia have been spared all colonizing attempts for the time being? Both of these would have been possibilities. What is certain is that the history of the region would have been different from the form which it has since taken.

That Acadia was not permanently abandoned by French colonization was owed in part to the actions of a single individual.

To be sure, those actions were heavily influenced by the same economic and political forces which had influenced de Monts. Yet the personal determination of the Baron de Poutrincourt to return to Port Royal was an important factor also. In early 1608, de Monts formally turned over to Poutrincourt the ownership of the building that had housed the colony, and planning began for a new expedition.

Poutrincourt faced major difficulties. First and foremost was the problem of finance. After the failure of de Monts' attempt in Acadia, merchant investors were not likely to come forward unless they could be convinced that the new venture would be more successful. Poutrincourt had no such evidence to offer, and accordingly commercial support did not materialize. Poutrincourt, however, had one advantage that de Monts had lacked. De Monts was a Protestant. Poutrincourt was a Catholic and could readily appeal for support to wealthy French Catholic sponsors on the ground that he intended to bring about the religious conversion of native people. From the beginning Poutrincourt used this as an argument in efforts to find private financing. Even so, the process was not easy.

In the summer of 1608, Poutrincourt believed that he had found a sponsor in the Bishop of Verdun, who was a powerful and wealthy aristocrat as well as being bishop. On the strength of this support, Poutrincourt bought and equipped a ship. Only then did he find out that a misunderstanding had somehow arisen: the bishop refused outright to pay the large bill presented by the outfitter of the ship. Without a source of support, and deep in debt, Poutrincourt did not even get as far as leaving the shores of France.[24]

After spending more than a year putting his finances back in order, Poutrincourt decided on a new strategy. He would invest heavily from his own resources, would send a ship to Acadia in early 1610, and would hope for success in both fur-trading and religious conversion. Using that success as an argument, he would then try again to obtain financial support.

Accordingly, Poutrincourt left the French port of Dieppe in February 1610. With him was his oldest son Charles de Biencourt, the priest Jessé Flesché, and about twenty other potential colonists. As in the case of the earlier settlement of de Monts, all were male. They included Claude and Charles de la Tour, a father and son who were later to play prominent roles in the evolution of Acadia. Following a long voyage, the Acadian coast was reached, and after a number of stops the ship arrived at Port Royal in June.

The habitation was intact. Guarded by Membertou and his Micmac band, it needed little more than repairs to the roof. The structure and the furnishings were exactly as Poutrincourt had left them in 1607. A new well had to be dug, and nearby land cleared for cultivation; then the settlement was apparently ready to take up where the previous colonists had left off three years before.

Yet matters were not quite so simple. Still to be resolved was the long-term financial position of the colony. Poutrincourt and his son, Biencourt, quickly set about implementing their strategy. As well as trading with native people for furs, they also prompted the religious conversion of Membertou and his family. Just three weeks after the arrival of the French expedition, Membertou and some twenty other Micmacs were baptized by Flesché. Shortly afterwards Biencourt departed for France with a shipload of furs and, as Champlain later recorded, "to carry the good news of the baptism of the savages."[25] The haste with which the whole series of events had taken place was no accident. It represented a deliberate effort to create quickly an impression of achievement both in trade and in religious conversion.[26]

The effort was partly successful. Biencourt arrived in France in the late summer of 1610 with two immediate objectives. One was to secure a monopoly of the fur trade on a similar basis to that of de Monts years before. The other, supported by the baptismal register brought from Port Royal, was to appeal for financial support from wealthy individuals in the cause of religious conversion. In this regard, Biencourt recruited Marc Lescarbot, the writer who had visited Acadia in 1606-07, to write an elaborate account of the baptism of Membertou and his family. Lescarbot accomplished the task within weeks. "The poor [native] people," he wrote, "groan for religious instruction"; he went on to threaten God's vengeance against those who "could help them to become Christians, and do not."[27] Obviously, the best way to avoid that vengeance was to contribute to Poutrincourt's treasury.

In his first purpose, Biencourt failed completely. To expect to be given a trade monopoly so soon after the cancellation of the similar privilege of de Monts was unrealistic. The support for religious conversion was more easily available, although not in the exact form Biencourt would have liked. When Biencourt arrived in France, King Henry IV had recently been assassinated by a religious opponent. He was succeeded by his nine-year-old son, Louis XIII, but real power was held for the time being by Henry's queen, Marie de Medici. The queen, who met with

Biencourt in early October 1610, had close connections with the powerful Jesuit religious order. The result was that Biencourt was put in contact with a potential sponsor in the person of the Marquise de Guercheville, a noblewoman who was also strongly pro-Jesuit. Agreement was reached in January 1611 that Guercheville would provide support on condition that Jesuit missionaries would take over the work of religious conversion in Acadia. Six days later, on 26 January 1611, Biencourt left Dieppe with 36 new colonists and the Jesuit missionaries Pierre Biard and Enemond Massé. [28]

The events following the arrival of Biencourt and his fellow voyagers at Port Royal in May 1611 obviously fall outside the decade of the 1600s. Acadia as a French colony had many remaining years of difficulty. Quarrels between Biencourt and the Jesuits would even lead to the splitting of the settlement into two in 1613, when the Jesuits left Port Royal to establish a mission near Mount Desert Island, on the coast of present-day Maine. Both that settlement and Port Royal were burned shortly afterwards by an English raiding party from Virginia. For many subsequent years, Biencourt, Charles de la Tour, and other colonists lived a tenuous life in Acadia, living on meagre profits from the fur trade and fishery. [29]

Yet the re-establishment of Acadian settlement by Poutrincourt in 1610, and Biencourt's efforts later in the year to obtain support in France, had marked a genuine turning-point. From 1610 onwards the French presence in the Maritime region was continuous. To be sure, Biencourt's sojourn in France was not completely successful. Not only did he fail in his quest for a trade monopoly, which might have brought benefits in the form of capital investment by merchants, but the intricate negotiations with Guercheville and the Jesuits delayed his intended departure for Port Royal from November 1610 to the following January. By the time he finally arrived back, Poutrincourt was on the point of abandoning the colony for lack of necessary supplies. Also, the presence of the Jesuits had only reluctantly been accepted by Biencourt. The Jesuits' first priority in Acadia was religious conversion rather than commercial profit, and in this they differed from Biencourt and his father. Their close connection with Guercheville gave the Jesuits a position of power, and this too would quickly become a divisive issue. [30]

Nevertheless, the arrival of the Jesuits had been a necessary price to pay for the survival of the colony. In the long term, the presence of religious missionaries in Acadia would prove to be an effective way of establishing cultural links with the native people whose support was essential to the survival of the colony. In the short term, the financial support obtained by Biencourt — and he ultimately managed to drive a good bargain with Guercheville and the Jesuits, involving a series of interest-free loans — made the difference between the survival or abandonment of the French colony in Acadia.

The colony in Acadia, however, could not survive only through the efforts of its French promoters. While the bare outline of events can be written — and all too often has been written — with the French at the centre and native people relegated to the fringes, this approach is not enough in itself to bring out one of the basic realities of the whole process. That reality is the power and influence of native people. Traditional histories of the Maritime region have allowed Indian people the role of assisting the colonists in times of difficulty. More recent research in Indian history reveals that their importance was much greater than that. Simply put, native people had the power in the decade of the 1600s to say "yes" or "no" to French colonization.

By the beginning of the decade, native peoples of the region, whether Micmac or Maliseet-Passamaquoddy, were continuing to struggle with the disastrous population decline that had so recently taken place. These native societies were still vital and coherent, and their resilience was seen clearly in their response to colonizing Europeans. The missionary Pierre Biard looked at Indian people with the biases that were characteristic of Europeans of his day, but he was too honest an observer to report the Indians' own attitudes in anything but a truthful way. Those attitudes surprised him. "You will see these poor barbarians . . .," he wrote on the basis of his experiences in Acadia, "holding their heads so high that they greatly underrate us, regarding themselves as our superiors." On another occasion, Biard wrote with some exasperation that "they think they are better, more valiant and ingenious than the French; and, what is difficult to believe, richer than we are."[31]

What Biard was finding out was that Indian people were not overwhelmingly impressed by the Europeans they met, including the French in Acadia. They did value some of the trappings of European society, especially goods such as metal tools, or glass beads that could be used for decorative purposes. The Europeans themselves, however, were seen as weak and sometimes foolish, especially in their stumbling efforts to cope with the North

American environment. Their appearance, especially those who had beards, was regarded as interesting but unattractive. Their materialism, as reflected in the lust for fur-trading profits, seemed vulgar to the native people, and so at times did their personal morality. Biard reported that native women were "very modest" and that once when "a certain madcap took some liberties," a Micmac delegation "came and told our our Captain that he should look out for his men, informing him that any one who attempted to do that again could not stand much of a chance, that they would kill him on the spot."[32]

Native people in Acadia, therefore, were fully able to appraise the French presence critically, and to assert the superiority of their own values when necessary. They also had considerable military force. To be sure, that force was not unified throughout the region, in that the Micmac and Maliseet-Passamaquoddy were separate peoples, and in that Micmac political and military organization was decentralized. Yet the Micmac held regular councils of chiefs, at which issues of war and peace were discussed. They were traditional allies of the Maliseet-Passamaquoddy. Furthermore, individual chiefs could themselves build impressive military power in their own localities. Membertou, for example, was known to be a formidable warrior. Given the small numbers of French present in the region, the fact was that they were there only as long as native people chose to tolerate them. They could just as easily have been killed or driven out, or simply left alone to struggle unsuccessfully with the North American climate and environment.[33]

There was also another side to the French dependence on native people. Aside from immediate questions of survival, the longer-term success of the colonial enterprise depended squarely on the colonists' ability to forge cooperative relationships with Indian people. Indians were the suppliers of the furs which were crucial to the commercial success of the colony. Trading relationships with the Micmac had obvious importance. Trade was also carried on on the opposite side of the Bay of Fundy from Port Royal, with the Maliseet. For this reason alone, the friendship of native people was necessarily courted by the French.

In the matter of religious conversion, the French also had a compelling need for Indian cooperation, especially during Poutrincourt's efforts to re-establish Acadian settlement in 1610. The need to demonstrate success in making Indian converts was central to the financial health of the colony. There could be no question, however, of making conversions by force or deception.

As in all other areas of interaction between Indians and colonists, native people approached the religious question from a position of strength. It was unlikely that any significant numbers would be found who would be willing to give up their own traditional beliefs for the doubtful benefits of a new religion preached by recently-arrived aliens.

Nevertheless, certain factors made religious conversion possible. One was the breadth of native religious beliefs. Native spirituality did not involve any one exclusive faith, but rather implied a belief in the power of a large number of spiritual forces. It was quite possible in that context to accept Christianity as one aspect of religious truth, while not abandoning more traditional beliefs. Also, religious conversion was often seen by native people as a means of symbolizing friendship or of cementing an alliance.[34]

The conversion of Membertou and his family in 1610 can best be seen in this context. Baptized only some three weeks after the arrival of the priest Flesché — who did not speak the Micmac language — these converts had not been given any elaborate course of instruction in the Christian religion. Pierre Biard later remarked specifically on the failure of Flesché to prepare potential converts thoroughly enough for baptism, and reported that Flesché himself had been glad to hand over his tasks to the Jesuits.[35] Be that as it may, the conversions of 1610 had served their purpose as far as Membertou and Poutrincourt were concerned: for Membertou, a sign of alliance and friendship renewed, as well as a means of access to a new aspect of the spiritual world; for Poutrincourt, also a symbol of alliance, as well as being a vital piece of evidence that the colony was serving a genuine religious purpose.

The importance of Membertou in sustaining the French presence in Acadia was profound. That importance has often been interpreted as stemming from Membertou's role as the amiable helper of the French. The truth was that Membertou's real significance for the French colonists was that he was an ally much more powerful than themselves. From the first arrival of the de Monts group at Port Royal in 1605, Membertou's support had offered a military guarantee as well as access to the necessary technology of survival in this part of North America. During the three years of French absence from Port Royal, it had been Membertou's Micmac band which had preserved the buildings of the settlement. When the French returned in 1610, it was the same chief and the same band who supplied the need for alliance and support, symbolized in religious conversion.

For the Micmac, the French presence was valued for very specific reasons. While native traditions of hospitality, and the personal friendship of Poutrincourt and Membertou, cannot be discounted as influential factors, the native interest in the French colony was not altruistic. European trade goods had an immediate economic and military value. As long as they were obtained only from short-term European visitors, the supply was not assured. When trade was conducted with a permanently-established habitation, this disadvantage no longer existed. The benefits of trade would apply especially to the Indian band in the immediate locality of the settlement. A chief such as Membertou would not only enjoy easy access to trade goods, but would also have the possibility of acting as an intermediary in trading those goods to other Indian people. For Membertou, as a powerful but aging leader, this was a strong attraction.

Had the Micmac had the power to see into the future, their decision might have been different. In the long term the fur trade had destructive effects on native society, which compounded the results of disease and the population decline that had already taken place. Yet in the context of the 1600s, the decision of the Micmac, and specifically that of Membertou, to accept the French presence was a rational response to prevailing circumstances. European trade goods could reasonably be seen at that time as strengthening native society rather than weakening it. Long experience in trading with visiting Europeans had given native people a shrewd appreciation of the value of their furs in terms of European products. Lescarbot later reported that the price of beaver in terms of such trade goods as knives had increased rapidly during the very years when the price of furs on the European market had also risen.[36] The Micmac had good reason to be self-confident in their ability to trade productively with the French.

Furthermore, a small settlement such as the one at Port Royal posed no evident threat of any kind to native people. On the contrary, it was so small and militarily so weak, that it needed the protection of native allies. Later events would show that even this small settlement was part of a much larger invasion of North America which would have disastrous results for native people. Although it would take another century and a half, the Micmacs themselves would ultimately be reduced to the status of a powerless minority. In the decade of the 1600s, however, it was clear that the French needed the Micmac more than the Micmac needed the French. Since there was no apparent reason to suppose that this would change, the toleration of French settlement — and even its encouragement, as by Membertou and his band — was neither rash nor foolish.

The decade of the 1600s represented a major turning-point in the human history of what is now the Maritime region. At the beginning of the decade, this was overwhelmingly the territory of native people. It was true that French and other European traders were arriving in increasing numbers for seasonal visits, and that the small and doomed French occupation of Sable Island had recently begun. Yet on the mainland, no non-native people lived in the region. By 1610, this was no longer true. To be sure, the impact of the Port Royal settlement should not be exaggerated. It too was very small, and as yet its French inhabitants were exclusively male. This in itself would emerge as a further element of the French-Micmac interaction, for stable family relationships could and did develop between the settlers and native women. Charles de la Tour and his Micmac wife, for example, had three daughters in the 1620s and early 1630s.[37] The immigration to Acadia of exclusively French family groups can be dated to the 1630s, and thus lay well in the future during the decade of the 1600s.

Yet the French presence in Acadia was continuous from 1610 onwards. The origin of that presence lay in the economic and political developments in France which had impelled de Monts to undertake Acadian settlement in 1604. Although the actual attempt of de Monts ended in failure in 1607, the effort of Poutrincourt to re-establish the colony was the direct descendant of that original venture. The later establishment of the Acadian people on the Bay of Fundy marshlands was, in turn, a development made possible by the persistence of the small colonial community established by Poutrincourt. Not only did the presence of Biencourt, La Tour, and others keep alive the economic interest of French merchants in this part of North America, but it was also one of the main arguments used by the French government to defend the French claim to ownership of Acadia against other competing European claims.[38] Had it not been for Poutrincourt's venture, the future of Acadia as a French colony would have been doubtful indeed.

What has all too often been overlooked by historians is the essential role played by native people in this entire process. In the decade of the 1600s, it was the native people of the region who held the real power. European colonizing attempts up and down the coasts of North America were small and fragile. They might succeed, but they often failed. Everywhere, the consequences of European success or failure were important to the subsequent course of history. Just as elsewhere, that was true in Acadia. The native peoples of the region, and especially the Micmac, could easily have eliminated the French colonial presence if they had chosen to do so. Some might argue in hindsight that they made a tragic mistake in tolerating any European settlement. Others would contend that, in the context of the massive European invasion of North America, it was to the Indians' benefit to support a form of colonization that was at least seemingly compatible with their own way of life.

What is certain is that, while the French and their leaders — de Monts, Champlain, Poutrincourt, and the others — were important participants in the events that took place, they were not in a position to determine the outcome. Native people, on the other hand, were in such a position. That they chose to offer toleration and support, particularly through the response of Membertou to the French presence at Port Royal, was essential to the persistence of French colonization. That choice was a crucial determining factor in a crucially important decade in the history of the region.

NOTES

1. See Robert E. Funk, "Post-Pleistocene Adaptations," in Bruce G. Trigger, ed., *Handbook of North American Indians, volume 15, Northeast* (Washington, 1978), pp. 16-17; James A. Tuck, "Regional Cultural Development 3000 to 300 B.C.," *ibid.*, p. 34.
2. T.J. Brasser, "Early European Contacts," *ibid.*, pp. 78-80; on changes prior to European contact, see James A. Tuck, *Maritime Provinces Prehistory* (Ottawa, 1984).
3. See Virginia Miller, "Aboriginal Micmac Population: A Review of the Evidence," *Ethnohistory*, 23 (1976), pp. 117-27.
4. *The Jesuit Relations and Allied Documents: Travels and Explorations of the Jesuit Missionaries in New France, 1610-1791*, ed. Reuben Gold Thwaites (73 vols.; Cleveland, 1896-1901), I, 177; III, 105.
5. See John G. Reid, *Acadia, Maine, and New Scotland: Marginal Colonies in the Seventeenth Century* (Toronto, 1981), pp. 4-5; for recent research findings, see David Sanger, "An Introduction in the Prehistory of the Passamaquoddy Bay Region," *American Review of Canadian Studies*, 16 (1986), pp. 139-59.
6. Reid, *Acadia, Maine, and New Scotland*, pp. 14-15; Marcel Trudel, *The Beginnings of New France, 1524-1663* (Toronto, 1973), pp. 83-4.
7. See Karen Ordahl Kupperman "The Puzzle of the American Climate in the Early Colonial Period," *American Historical Review*, 87 (1982), pp. 1262-89.
8. Henry Percival Biggar, ed., *The Works of Samuel de Champlain* (6 vols.; Toronto, 1922-36), I, 307.
9. Trudel, *Beginnings*, pp. 86-7; George MacBeath, "Pierre Du Gua de Monts," *Dictionary of Canadian Biography*, (hereafter DCB), (9 vols. to date; Toronto, 1966-   ), I, 292-3.
10. See Lucien Campeau, "Henri Membertou," DCB, I, 500-1.
11. See Huia Ryder *et al.*, "Jean de Biencourt de Poutrincourt et de Saint-Just," DCB, I, 96-9.
12. *Ibid.*
13. Gabriel Sagard, quoted in Marcel Trudel, *The Beginnings of New France,*

1524-1663 (Toronto, 1973), p. 88; on the probable accuracy of the story, see Elizabeth Jones, *Gentlemen and Jesuits: Quests for Glory and Adventure in the Early Days of New France* (Toronto, 1986), p. 68.

14. Marc Lescarbot, *The History of New France . . .* , ed. W.L. Grant (3 vols.; Toronto, 1907-14), II, 344.

15. Biggar, *Works of Champlain,* I, 447.

16. Robert Le Blant, "Le commerce compliquée des fourrures canadiennes au début du XVIIe siècle," *Revue d'histoire de l'Amérique française,* 26 (1972-3), pp. 56-7.

17. Reid, *Acadia, Maine and New Scotland,* pp. 15-18; MacBeath, "De Monts," DCB, I, 293.

18. Gustave Lanctot, "Troilus de la Roche de Mesgouez," DCB, I, 421-2.

19. See Reid, *Acadia, Maine, and New Scotland,* pp. 6-7.

20. Trudel, *Beginnings,* pp. 34-53.

21. See John G. Reid, "The Scots Crown and the Restitution of Port Royal, 1629-1632," *Acadiensis,* 6, No. 2 (Spring 1977), pp. 39-40.

22. William Strachey, "History of travaile into Virginia," in Henry O. Thayer, ed., *The Sagadahoc Colony,* (Portland, Me., 1892), p. 85; David B. Quinn, *North America from Earliest Discovery to First Settlements: The Norse Voyages to 1612* (New York, 1977), pp. 439-64; Gillian T. Cell, *English Enterprise in Newfoundland, 1577-1660* (Toronto, 1969), pp. 53-80; Reid, *Acadia, Maine, and New Scotland,* pp. 15-18.

23. Sir Ferdinando Gorges, "Brief Relation," in Henry Sweetser Burrage, ed., *Gorges and the Grant of the Province of Maine* (Portland, Me., 1923), p. 142.

24. Lucien Campeau, ed., *Monumentae Novae Franciae, vol. I: la première mission d'Acadie* (Quebec and Rome, 1967), Introduction, pp. 191-3.

25. Biggar, *Works of Champlain,* IV, 4.

26. Trudel, *Beginnings,* pp. 107-8; Campeau, "Membertou," DCB, I, 500-01.

27. Translated from Marc Lescarbot, "La Conversion des Sauvages," in Campeau, *Première mission,* p. 86.

28. Trudel, *Beginnings,* pp. 108-11; Campeau, *Première mission,* Introduction, pp. 195-210.

29. See Reid, *Acadia, Maine, and New Scotland,* p. 19.

30. Trudel, *Beginnings,* pp. 111-114.

31. *Jesuit Relations,* I, 173; III, 75.

32. *Jesuit Relations,* III, 103-5.

33. Philip K. Bock, "Micmac," Trigger, *Handbook, vol. 15,* p. 116; Campeau, "Membertou," DCB, I, 500.

34. Reid, *Acadia, Maine, and New Scotland,* pp. 74-5.

35. Campeau, "Membertou," DCB, I, 500-1; Campeau, *Première mission,* pp. 139-40.

36. See Cornelius J. Jaenen, "Amerindian Views of French Culture in the Seventeenth Century," *Canadian Historical Review,* 55 (1976), p. 267.

37. George MacBeath, "Charles de Saint-Etienne de la Tour," DCB, I, 595; M.A. MacDonald, *Fortune and La Tour: The Civil War in Acadia* (Toronto, 1983), pp. 13, 43.

38. See Reid, "Scots Crown and the Restitution of Port Royal," pp. 39-63.

FURTHER
READING

For the decade of the 1600s, a number of excellent original sources have survived, and have been made widely available in published English translations. There are three major authors who give first-hand accounts of life in Acadia at this time: Samuel de Champlain, in H.P. Biggar, ed., *The Works of Samuel de Champlain* (6 vols.; Champlain Society, Toronto, 1922-36); Marc Lescarbot, *The History of New France*, ed. W.L. Grant (3 vols.; Champlain Society, Toronto, 1907-14); and the works of Pierre Biard, in R.G. Thwaites, ed., *The Jesuit Relations and Allied Documents* (73 vols.; Burrows Brothers, Cleveland, Ohio, 1896-1901), volumes I-IV. All three comment on native societies as well as French colonization, with the observations of Biard especially useful, and all three can be read with pleasure by the general reader as well as the specialized scholar.

Many historians have written on the development of French colonization in Acadia during the decade of the 1600s. The following books contain English language accounts offering a variety of perspectives: H.P. Biggar, *The Early Trading Companies of New France* (University of Toronto, Toronto 1901); Andrew Hill Clark, *Acadia: The Geography of Early Nova Scotia to 1760* (University of Wisconsin Press, Madison, 1968); Naomi Griffiths, *The Acadians: Creation of a People* (McGraw-Hill Ryerson, Toronto, 1973); Elizabeth Jones, *Gentlemen and Jesuits: Quests for Glory and Adventure in the Early Days of New France* (University of Toronto Press [hereafter UTP], Toronto, 1986); D.B. Quinn, *North America from Earliest Discovery to First Settlements* (Harper and Row, New York, 1977); J.G. Reid, *Acadia, Maine, and New Scotland: Marginal Colonies in the Seventeenth Century* (UTP, Toronto, 1981); and Marcel Trudel, *The Beginnings of New France, 1524-1663* (McClelland and Stewart, Toronto, 1973). Also a major source is the *Dictionary of Canadian Biography*, Volume I (UTP, Toronto, 1966).

Naturally, there are also many French-language accounts of these events. Especially useful is Marcel Trudel, *Histoire de la Nouvelle-France: le comptoir, 1604-1627* (Fides, Montreal, 1966), which is a fuller account

than appears in the same author's *Beginnings of New France*, listed above.
An older work is Emile Lauvrière, *La tragédie d'un peuple: histoire du peuple
acadien de ses origines à nos jours* (2 vols; Bossard, Paris, 1922). An
important author whose works are not so easy to locate in non-specialized
libraries is Robert Le Blant: see, for example, his "Le commerce compliqué
des fourrures canadiennes au début du XVIIe siècle," in *Revue d'histoire
de l'Amérique française*, 26 (1972-3), pp. 53-66.

On the history of native people at this time, a good starting point
is the pioneering study of A.G. Bailey, *The Conflict of European and Eastern
Algonkian Cultures, 1504-1700* (2nd ed.; UTP, Toronto, 1969). The works
of Cornelius J. Jaenen are also essential: *Friend and Foe: Aspects of French-
Amerindian Cultural Contacts in the Sixteenth and Seventeenth Centuries*
(McClelland and Stewart, Toronto, 1976); and "Amerindian Views of
French Culture in the Seventeenth Century," in *Canadian Historical Review*,
55 (1974), pp. 261-91. A concise account of changes in Micmac society
is given by H.F. McGee, Jr., "The Micmac Indians: The Earliest Migrants,"
in D.F. Campbell, ed., *Banked Fires: The Ethnics of Nova Scotia* (Scribblers'
Press, Port Credit, Ont., 1978). Other relevant material can be found in
various articles in Bruce G. Trigger, ed., *Handbook of North American
Indians, Volume 15, Northeast* (Smithsonian Institution, Washington, 1978),
and in James A. Tuck, *Maritime Provinces Prehistory* (National Museums
of Canada, Ottawa, 1984); see also the reappraisal offered in David Sanger,
"An Introduction to the Prehistory of the Passamaquoddy Bay Region,"
American Review of Canadian Studies, 16 (1986), pp. 139-59. A stimulating
although controversial interpretation of the Micmac response to European
influences can be found in Calvin Martin, *Keepers of the Game* (University
of California Press, Berkeley, 1978). A more general approach to the
history of Indian-European relations in the region is offered by the articles
contained in H.F. McGee, Jr., *The Native Peoples of Atlantic Canada*
(Carleton University Press, Ottawa, 1983).

THE
1750s:
DECADE OF
EXPULSION

In the 140 years separating the end of the decade of the 1600s from the beginning of the 1750s much had changed in the Maritime region. Native people no longer comprised the majority of the population, and had not done so since approximately 1720 when the Acadian population overtook that of the Indian peoples. The Acadians themselves were French-speaking and were largely of French origin, although there were also individuals and families from other European nations who had been assimilated over the years: Scots, Irish, Portuguese. While the origins of the French presence in Acadia can be traced to the decade of the 1600s, the direct ancestors of the Acadian people had, for the most part, settled on the Fundy marshlands during the 1630s and 1640s.

The Acadian experience had been eventful from the start. During the 1640s a brief but destructive conflict between rival colonial promoters — Charles de la Tour and Charles de Menou d'Aulnay — had threatened disruption of the main Acadian settlement at Port Royal. The following decade saw the colony conquered and occupied by English forces, to be restored to France by treaty only after sixteen years of English rule. War between France and England was renewed in 1690, and once again Acadia came under attack. In 1710, Port Royal was captured by the English — or rather by the British, since the two kingdoms of England and Scotland had united in 1707. The conquest of Acadia was confirmed by the Treaty of Utrecht in 1713, and the majority of the Acadian people would henceforth be a French population on British territory.

Yet not all. The treaty of 1713 did not turn over to Great Britain the whole of the area now known as the Maritime provinces. Cape Breton Island, renamed Ile Royale, and Prince Edward Island, which was still known by its original French designation of Ile Saint-Jean, were to be retained by France. Some Acadians, though only a small proportion, chose at various times after 1713 to move from the mainland to one or other of those islands. On the fate of the mainland territories, the treaty was ambiguous. Nobody disputed that the modern peninsular Nova Scotia was to be owned by Great Britain. The status of the modern New Brunswick was more doubtful, as the treaty said only that Britain would have possession of Acadia "with its ancient boundaries."[1]

For the Acadians in 1713, however, this was no more than a technicality. The fact was that the major Acadian settlements were now undoubtedly located in the British colony of Nova Scotia. They included Port Royal, now renamed Annapolis Royal, and clusters of settlements around the Minas Basin, on Cobequid Bay, and on the Isthmus of Chignecto.

How would the Acadian communities respond to their new situation? In one sense, Acadians had a great deal of relevant experience. The violent conflicts of the previous century had created a strong tradition of adaptability and political pragmatism as Acadians tried to survive as a coherent society despite conflicting French and English claims to rule the colony. In part this meant maintaining effective though informal structures of local community government. As early as 1679 Governor Frontenac of New France commented critically on the Acadians' slowness to obey orders without first discussing them in an independent spirit. For him, this reflected their "parliamentary tendency."[2] Acadian strategies also included the maintaining of trade links with both English and French. Even while under French rule, Acadians carried on a flourishing illegal trade with New England merchants. "Every year," reported a French official in 1697, "the English bring to these places trade-goods . . . , taking in exchange pelts and grain."[3] Thus Acadians proved well able to take independent attitudes to complex situations.[4]

Following the Treaty of Utrecht, this pragmatism evolved into a more explicit strategy of neutrality between British and French. To repeated demands that they take an oath of allegiance to Great Britain, Acadian community leaders consistently replied that they would only do so on certain conditions. Prime among the conditions was that they not be expected to fight against their French former compatriots in the event of another war. In the late 1720s, many Acadians did sign an oath of allegiance, maintaining that the British governor of the day had given them verbal assurance that their neutrality would be respected. The existence

Acadian dyke-building, by Azor Vienneau

of any such condition would later be disputed by the British. For the time being, however, it seemed that the principle of Acadian neutrality had been established.[5]

With this question apparently resolved, the Acadian economy expanded as years went by. Fundy marshlands were steadily reclaimed and used for both crops and livestock farming. Trade was carried on both with the New England colonies and (illegally) with French Canada and the Cape Breton fortress of Louisbourg. The Acadian population expanded from some 2,500 at the time of the Treaty of Utrecht to at least 10,000 by 1750.[6] A British surveyor, Charles Morris, commented strikingly in a document written about 1749 on the appearance of mellow prosperity that struck him when visiting the Acadian community of Beaubassin on the Isthmus of Chignecto:

> Here may be seen a Number of Villages built on gentle rising Hills interspers'd with long intervalls of marshes and they at a great distance bounded by Hills covered with Trees, the Natural growth of the Country; here may be seen Rivers turning and winding among the Marshes, then Cloath'd with all the Variety of Grain.[7]

For all this apparently stable development, however, there was also a darker side to the Acadian situation at this time. The severing of the connection with other French societies had had its effect in areas such as education, and illiteracy rates had grown since the conquest. New immigration into the communities had also declined drastically since 1713, and there was a clear danger that a more inward-looking Acadian society would result.[8] Most immediately threatening of all was the question of whether the Acadian strategy of neutrality could survive in an era of increasing tension between the two rival powers, France and Great Britain.

As the year 1750 opened, the position of the Acadians was becoming more complicated because of the increasing militarization of the region. Just six years earlier, France and Great Britain had again gone to war. Although primarily a European conflict, this four-year war had left a considerable legacy of bitterness in North America. On the east coast the major battle had been the conquest of Fortress Louisbourg by New England forces in 1745. A French effort to mount a naval counter-attack had been a disastrous failure. Not so was an expedition of 680

Canadian militia, which left Quebec for Nova Scotia in the late spring of 1746. Commanded by the Sieur de Ramezay, the force did not succeed in taking Annapolis Royal, but did inflict defeat on a 500-strong detachment of New England troops at Grand Pré in a night attack in February 1747.[9]

The Treaty of Aix-la-Chapelle in 1748 put an end to armed conflict for the time being. Yet it did nothing to contribute to lasting peace. No effort was made in the treaty to resolve the dispute over the status of the territory of the modern New Brunswick. The only major provision affecting North America, in fact, was the return of Louisbourg to France, in exchange for the return to Britain of Madras, in India. The news of this British concession of Louisbourg was received in New England with a sense of betrayal. New England troops had won a great and costly victory, according to the popular view, only to be "Vanquish'd by Peace."[10]

If many New Englanders looked bitterly on the French return to the Ile Royale, their bitterness was also turned towards the Acadians. Allegations were made by survivors of the February 1747 battle at Grand Pré that Acadians had not only provisioned the Canadian troops and acted as scouts for them, but in some cases had actually taken part in the attack and had killed a number of New Englanders. There were suggestions too that Acadians had given assistance to Micmac and Maliseet forces in earlier unsuccessful attacks on Annapolis Royal, in 1744.[11] A quite different emphasis was evident in the verdict of Nova Scotia's lieutenant-governor and military commander, Paul Mascarene. While Mascarene freely admitted that some Acadians had co-operated with French and Indian attackers, he credited the successful defence of the province — of Annapolis Royal in particular — to the strict adherence of most Acadians to their position of neutrality. The French, Mascarene reported had "us'd all the means of cajoling and threatning to make them take up arms ... [but] they could not prevail above twenty to join with them."[12]

Be that as it might, the conflicts of the 1740s had posed a severe threat to the Acadian strategy of neutrality. The building of fortifications throughout the region after the peace treaty gave little hope that the pressure would slacken. The French force that reoccupied Louisbourg arrived at almost exactly the same time in late July 1749 as a British military and colonizing expedition landed at Chebucto Bay, on the Atlantic coast of Nova Scotia, to establish the town of Halifax and its citadel. Two months before, Canadian troops under the Sieur de Boishébert had reasserted the

French claim to the modern New Brunswick by raising the flag at the mouth of the St. John River, just across the Bay of Fundy from the former British headquarters at Annapolis Royal.[13] Despite the formal establishment of peace in 1748, this was a time of preparation for war.

The preparations continued rapidly in 1750. Another Canadian force, under Louis de La Corne, had taken up a position on the Isthmus of Chignecto in late 1749, again asserting the French territorial claim. In April 1750, British troops under Major Charles Lawrence landed on the isthmus. Temporarily frustrated by the superior numbers of the French, Lawrence soon withdrew; but in September he returned to build a fort in the area known thenceforth as Fort Lawrence. Early in 1751, the French built their own fortification — Fort Beauséjour — a few hundred metres to the west. Separated only by low-lying marsh and the tiny Missaguash river, the representatives of the world's two most expansionist empires looked warily at one another, and waited.

The Acadians had already been directly affected. Prior to Lawrence's arrival in the spring of 1750, the Acadian community of Beaubassin had been visited by Micmac fighters accompanied by the French priest and missionary Jean-Louis Le Loutre. Le Loutre has often been cast in the role of the villain of the entire series of events of the 1750s. Lawrence too has been portrayed as such, by other writers. More recent historical interpretations have been justifiably sceptical of the notion that individual villainy can explain what was to take place. That these two were influential participants, however, is not in dispute. The events of early 1750, and Le Loutre's role in them, are clouded by the lack of conclusive surviving evidence. Le Loutre certainly attempted to persuade the Acadians of Beaubassin to move across the marsh to the French territory. The Acadians did move, and their homes were then burned by the Micmac shortly before Lawrence landed. But the removal was probably prompted by threats, possibly by outright force.[14]

The Beaubassin Acadians became refugees. Some would continue for several years to live on the fringes of Fort Beauséjour. Others would continue their journey to the apparently more secure French territory of the Ile Saint-Jean. There they joined with other Acadians who had been moving in increasing numbers to the island since the beginning of 1750. Of a total population of 2223 revealed by a census of 1752, no fewer than 1188 had immigrated in 1750 or 1751.[15] Events would prove that this refuge was not a secure one. That the migrations took place, however, was an indication of the pressures felt by Acadians at this time.

Fort Lawrence, 1755

The pressure had been increased in the spring of 1751, when an official order was made known in the communities that "all Acadians who (within eight days of the publication of this) have not taken the oath of fidelity and are not incorporated within the Militia companies which we have created, will be declared rebels . . . and as such expelled from the lands which they hold."[16] The order came not from the British, but from the Marquis de La Jonquière, governor of New France. The British military government of Nova Scotia had not yet threatened expulsion, though the possibility had been privately discussed during the war of the 1740s, but Governor Edward Cornwallis was known to be intent on resuming the British effort to procure from the Acadians an unconditional oath of allegiance. For the time being, he was restrained by orders from London not to take any measures that might prompt further Acadian out-migration from Nova Scotia, but the double threat to the Acadians — from French and British alike — was clear enough.[17]

The Acadians were not the only civilian population to be living under threat of military force in Nova Scotia. When Cornwallis had arrived in 1749, he had brought more than 2500 settlers to the new town named after the president of the British Board of Trade, Lord Halifax. By the end of the following year, following immigration by New Englanders and by the first group of "Foreign Protestants" — Swiss, German, and French settlers recruited by the British government — the population had swelled to some 5000.[18]

While the French had no reason to welcome this influx of settlers to Nova Scotia, which represented the first major non-Indian and non-Acadian group to live there, they also had no basis on which to object. By the Treaty of Utrecht this was British territory. The Micmac, however, had never been consulted about the treaty, and had never accepted its provisions. In 1720, a Micmac raiding party had burned a British ship at anchor in Minas Basin, and a captured member of the group had made a revealing declaration: "This land here that God has given to us . . . cannot be disputed by anyone. ... We are masters independent of everyone and wish to have our country free."[19] With the Acadians, the Micmac had a close and long-standing relationship, even though the circumstances of the burning of Beaubassin may indicate that military considerations were capable of weakening this tie. With the French, the Micmac were allied though never in a subservient role. With the British, despite occasional temporary truces and treaties, the Micmac considered themselves at war, as against an illegitimate occupying power.

Hence the constant Micmac pressure on Halifax during the first three years of its existence. Although native forces were never strong enough to mount a successful attack on the town itself, the settlers were virtually confined within its boundaries, and even Dartmouth — on the other side of the harbour — was effectively Micmac territory. The Foreign Protestants had been intended for settlement on the Isthmus of Chignecto and the shores of Minas Basin, with the purpose of beginning a process of non-Acadian immigration into these areas that would ultimately bring about the assimilation of the Acadians into a larger Nova Scotia population. Until 1753, however, this group was unable to leave Halifax. By that time, when the military power of Halifax had grown to the point where effective protection could be offered, a new site had been selected and the founding of the town of Lunenburg was the result. Lunenburg was close enough to Halifax to be readily defended, and also so that the potentially mutinous settlers — soured by their experiences in Halifax — could be kept under supervision. Even so the town continued to be vulnerable to the Micmac, and as late as 1758 underwent an effective surprise raid launched by a French and Micmac force from a base on the Ile Saint-Jean.[20]

Naturally the British authorities and settlers in Nova Scotia took a very different view of the Indian raids from that taken by the Micmac themselves. For the Nova Scotia council in 1749, the Micmac were to be regarded as "Rebels to His Majesty's Government or as so many Banditte Ruffians and treated accordingly." A bounty was thereupon offered for every Indian scalped or captured alive, whether man, woman, or child.[21] That such an order was given was an indication of the remaining military power of the Micmac, and of its successful exercise. The order also indicated a fear and bitterness on the part of the British that would bode ill for native people if ever buttressed by superior military force. That the French, including the Acadians, were regarded by the Nova Scotia military government as natural allies of the Micmac was another indication of the possible direction that future conflict might take.

War in North America was already well advanced by the time France and Great Britain made formal declaration in 1756. By that time, the destruction of the Acadian communities on the Bay of Fundy was complete. Two years later, the elimination of

France as a colonial power in the region would be effected by the British capture of Ile Royale and Ile Saint-Jean. The more general defeat of French forces in North America would come in 1759 and 1760, with British rule over the former French colonies to be confirmed by the Treaty of Paris in 1763.

The direct origins of the renewal of warfare in Nova Scotia were twofold. Skirmishes between French and Anglo-American forces in the Ohio Valley in the summer of 1754 led in the following year to the dispatch of British regular troops to Virginia under the command of General Edward Braddock. As commander-in-chief in North America, Braddock carried instructions that included co-operating with Lawrence on an attack on Fort Beauséjour.[22] Lawrence was by this time acting as governor of Nova Scotia, although not yet formally appointed. The actual governor, Peregrine Hopson, had left Nova Scotia in late 1753 because of ill health and Lawrence had taken over his duties with the title of president of the council. In that capacity, he had corresponded with the governor of Massachusetts, William Shirley, and in this correspondence lay the second direct origin of the renewal of war.

Shirley, like many New Englanders, was convinced that the French presence in the Maritime region was a major threat to New England, and that the Acadian population in Nova Scotia had to be considered part of the threat unless the Acadians took an unconditional oath of allegiance to Great Britain. In 1754, he suggested a strategy to Lawrence. New England forces should attack Fort Beauséjour in the following year, both as a first step to a conquest of Louisbourg and as an end in itself. Once Beauséjour was taken, New England settlers would be shipped in to the Isthmus of Chignecto and points further west, in order to make good the British claim to the modern New Brunswick. If the Acadians of the area chose to stay on British terms, they could do so. Otherwise they would have to move. By early 1755 the plan had evolved, though it was not yet precisely defined. The Chignecto Acadians would not, for the time being, be offered the chance to take the oath of allegiance. Lawrence suspected, he wrote to his chief military commander, Robert Monckton, that it might become necessary "to extirpate them."[23]

Thus, with a plan that included a possible removal of Acadians from the Chignecto area, but implied no general expulsion, the expedition against Fort Beauséjour set sail from Boston on 19 May 1755. It included a small force of British regular troops and almost 2000 New England militiamen. By contrast, Fort Beauséjour had

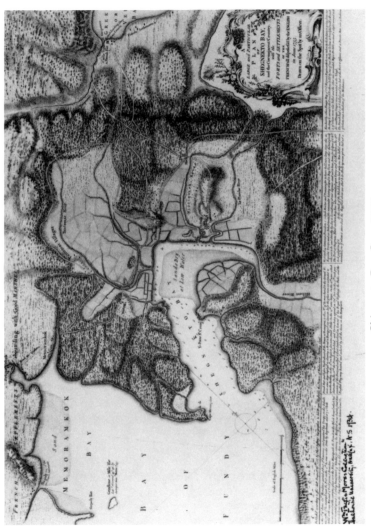

Chignecto Bay, June 1755

a garrison of 160. For all that, the conquest would not necessarily be easy. The fort had a commanding position above the marsh, and adequate artillery. A frontal assault would be costly and uncertain of success, and so a lengthy siege was a strong possibility. Monckton, however, chose to test the French defences by marching up the Missaguash River to a crossing at Pont à Buot, and then advancing down Beauséjour ridge to take up a position overlooking the fort. Despite resistance from a small French and Indian force at the river crossing, the tactic succeeded and on 14 June the British artillery opened fire directly on Fort Beauséjour. With panic growing in the fort, and after word had come from Louisbourg that no relief expedition was possible, the French commander surrendered on 16 June. A smaller neighbouring fort on Baie Verte, Fort Gaspereau, was surrendered the following day without a shot being fired.[24]

The fall of Fort Beauséjour did not bring to an end the formal military conflict between French and British in the Maritime region. Skirmishes continued to be fought, involving the French force commanded by the Sieur de Boishébert, based on the St. John River and later (in 1757 and 1758) on the Mirimachi River, further north in present-day New Brunswick.[25] In 1758, however, came the final conquests of Ile Royale, including the capture of Louisbourg, and of Ile Saint-Jean. From that time forward, except for the declining power of native people, Great Britain enjoyed virtually exclusive control of the region.

Yet in late June of 1755, these subsequent conquests were only vague future plans, and the chief focus of the Nova Scotia council's attention was on the Isthmus of Chignecto. At this point it was becoming evident that the conquest of Fort Beauséjour itself, despite its meticulous military execution, had been only vaguely planned. The notion of sending New England settlers to the area soon had to be abandoned, as no effective arrangements had been made either to recruit the potential settlers or to survey the available land and make land grants. Charles Lawrence had no orders from London to cover the situation. The Beauséjour expedition, although authorized in general terms by Braddock's instructions, had been carried out without the direct knowledge of the British government. Lawrence had even paid for the venture by using, without authorization, the money supplied by Britain for the general administration of Nova Scotia.[26] The situation, in short, was confused. About certain facts, however, there was no confusion: namely, that after the unexpectedly quick demise of Fort Beauséjour, Lawrence and his commanders had available a large army, a large transport fleet, and at least three months of good campaigning weather. How these resources would be used was yet to be determined.

From this point onwards, matters moved rapidly towards the expulsion from Nova Scotia of a large proportion of the Acadian people. As with many major historical turning-points, the origins lay in the operation of strong conflicting forces. In this case, the conflict of two expanding imperial systems, British and French, was the precondition for the deportation of the Acadians. Yet again, as with other crucial episodes of change, the direction ultimately taken by the events was not necessarily the only possible result. A series of developments during the summer of 1755, profoundly influenced by misunderstanding and misjudgement, would bring about the destruction of the existing Acadian communities of Nova Scotia.

Essential to this sequence of events was the perception of the Acadians by the British in Nova Scotia, and especially by Lawrence and the council. For many years British attitudes to the Acadians had been ambivalent. Even among government and military officers, two very different views had been evident. That it was highly unusual to have a predominantly French population in a British colony went without saying. That the Acadian population could have a strategic influence in favour of the French was also clear, but this would only be true if significant numbers of Acadians decided to work actively on behalf of the French in a time of war. If this did not happen, the Acadian presence had clear benefits for the British. The Acadians, for the time being, were the only large agriculturally-based population that Nova Scotia had and they were also active in other important pursuits such as the fishery. In due course British settlers might be recruited to live side-by-side with the Acadians, and eventually assimilate them. In the short term, though, any removal of the Acadians — forced or unforced — would have an economic cost, and might also strengthen the French by adding to the population of the Ile Royale and the Ile Saint-Jean.

Hence the two possible perceptions. The first was that the Acadians were a military threat to Great Britain, and always had been. Influenced by priests sent from Louisbourg and Quebec, and allied with the Micmac, the Acadians (according to this view) had shown their true colours in the 1740s by contributing to the French war effort at that time. Thus, the argument concluded, the only realistic options were either for the Acadians to declare immediate unconditional allegiance to Great Britain, or for them to be removed from Nova Scotia whenever circumstances permitted. The second perception was based on a recognition that some Acadians had fought for France in the 1740s. What was more significant, however, was that the majority had not done so. To be sure, they should all take an unconditional oath of allegiance at some future time, probably when the formal French presence in Cape Breton had been eliminated. Yet for those who argued this way, there was no reason whatever why the Acadian population should not eventually become a settled and productive part of the overall population of the province, and certainly no reason to disrupt the economy by forcing them to move.

This latter view had been held by two of the recent governing officers of Nova Scotia. Paul Mascarene had argued the case strongly during the 1740s. Peregrine Hopson, like Mascarene a professional military officer and the predecessor of Charles Lawrence as governor of Nova Scotia, took a similar approach. As late as July 1753 he argued to the British government that as soon as the French and Indian threat had been removed, the Acadians "will take the oaths, and . . . enjoy the benefit of English laws and liberty, and that Agriculture will flourish and enable us not only to maintain ourselves, but to carry on a very large and advantageous fishery at a reasonable rate."[27] After Hopson's departure from the province in November 1753, however, it was the other view of the Acadians that predominated, both in the mind of Lawrence and in the prevailing assumptions of his council.

There was ambivalence too among the Acadians. The predominant srategy was still that of neutrality. In 1753, for example, a large group of the Beaubassin Acadians still encamped at Fort Beauséjour had complained of ill treatment by the French, and requested British permission to move back to their old lands across the marsh. That they were refused this permission, except on condition of taking an unconditional oath of allegiance, and that the French commander also refused them permission to leave, does not obscure the reality that this was a further effort by Acadians to live life independently of the conflicts taking place around them.[28] In a similar vein, a petition of 25 Acadians of the Minas district as late as 10 June 1755 assured Lawrence that they would adhere strictly to the terms of the conditional oath of allegiance they had taken years before, and that there was therefore no need for them to surrender their hunting weapons, as recently ordered by the Nova Scotia council.[29]

Other Acadians, though a much lesser proportion, had decided to abandon the position of neutrality. One who had long done so was Joseph Brossard, known as Beausoleil. Brossard had assisted the French forces in the night battle at Grand Pré in 1747, and at the siege of Beauséjour he again emerged as a strong partisan of the French cause by leading a series of raids on the British positions. Brossard was not a resident of the Nova Scotia Acadian communities, having moved about 1740 to a new settlement in today's Albert County, New Brunswick, in French-claimed territory. It seems clear that a number of the Beaubassin Acadians fought with him at Beauséjour although the evidence also suggests that most Acadians refused to participate in the battle, even when summoned to do so by the French commander, the Sieur de Vergor. A number of those who did carry arms had Vergor sign a declaration saying he had forced them to do so, and the formal surrender of the fort — a document signed by both Monckton and Vergor — specified that they would be pardoned by the British for that reason.[30]

That promised pardon was never given. The presence of some 300 Acadians in the fort, though not all carrying arms, was interpreted by Lawrence as a provocation. The case of the other Acadian communities was taken up by the Nova Scotia council in July. On the 3rd, the Minas petitioners were summoned to appear before the council to explain their "insolent" response to the order to surrender their firearms. Ultimately, after extensive questioning, they were ordered to take an unconditional oath of allegiance or face unspecified consequences. They refused, at least until they had returned to the community for discussions. This was, the council minutes recorded, an "extraordinary Reply."[31] Nevertheless, it remained the Acadians' response until, later in the month, new representatives were called to Halifax from the Minas area and from Annapolis Royal. At meetings on the 25th and 28th the Acadian deputies again promised to adhere to their conditional oath, but again refused to take the new, unconditional oath. On the same day, the 28th, the chief justice of Nova Scotia, Jonathan Belcher, drew up a legal opinion to the effect that the Acadians "to this day . . . have appeared in no other light than that of Rebels to His Majesty," and concluded that he was "obliged . . . to advise that all the French [Acadian] Inhabitants may be removed from the Province."[32]

The expulsion of the Acadians began on the Isthmus of Chignecto on August 11th. All Acadians in the area were summoned to Fort Beauséjour — now renamed Fort Cumberland — and were imprisoned there prior to being ordered on board ships bound for the British-American colonies further south.

Similar measures were taken soon afterwards in the Minas Basin settlements and at Annapolis Royal, and by December the majority of the Nova Scotia Acadians had been deported. There was resistance, especially in areas on the New Brunswick side of the isthmus where Boishébert and his Canadian troops could provide support. Some Acadians found opportunities to escape the expulsion by removal or simply by taking refuge in the woods. Nevertheless, some 7000 Acadians were deported by year's end.[33]

Moreover, the deportations continued for years afterward. The British capture of Ile Royale and Ile Saint-Jean in 1758 prompted the expulsion of perhaps another 2000 Acadians, and probably 1000 more were taken in smaller groups between 1755 and 1762. Some Acadians succeeded in fleeing to Canada, and found safety there even in spite of the British conquest of 1759-60. In Nova Scotia by 1761, Jonathan Belcher estimated that just over 1500 Acadians were still at large. Many of them had taken refuge in the northern part of the modern New Brunswick, and about 800 were captured there later in the same year.[34] Absolute statistical precision is impossible to attain. What is clear, though, is that the old Acadian communities had been destroyed for ever.

To assess an event, or series of events, such as the Acadian expulsion is no easy task. The difficulty is reflected in the number of historians who have taken refuge in emotional and simplistic arguments to explain what happened. Some have suggested that the expulsion can be attributed solely to the evil character and wanton cruelty of Charles Lawrence. Others have written just as harshly of the missionary Jean-Louis Le Loutre, as the unscrupulous French agent who led the Acadians tragically astray. Yet recent historical writing has shown persuasively that there is nothing in the biography of either individual to suggest such personal depravity as a cause of the expulsion, despite the fact that each was much more warlike in his patriotic cause than were the Acadians as a people.[35] Complex historical questions cannot be resolved by simplistic answers.

Any adequate assessment must begin with the recognition that the expulsion was a human catastrophe for the Acadian people. It is true that deliberately abusive treatment of Acadian deportees was not so evident in 1755 as in the 1758 phase of the expulsion, when the conquests of Ile Royale and Ile Saint-Jean were carried out with undoubted brutality. It was in that year, for example, that some 700 Acadians from Ile Saint-Jean perished when their overloaded ships foundered at sea.[36] Yet even in 1755 the record

Acadian house in flames, by Azor Vienneau

was not free of acts of cruelty beyond what might have been regarded as the call of duty. Conditions varied from place to place. At Grand Pré, for example, the New England militia officer John Winslow apparently took pains to carry out his orders with as much humanity as possible, in supervising the expulsion from that area.[37] On the isthmus, meanwhile, Monckton was ordered by Lawrence in September that "I would have you not wait for the Wives and Children coming in but ship off the Men without them."[38] Separation of families was not a general policy during the expulsion, but there is no doubt that it happened even within nuclear families and very often within the extended families that were characteristic of Acadian society.

More generally, the ruination of the Acadian communities was virtually complete. An exception such as Memramcook, a small community just to the west of the isthmus where Boishébert's Canadian troops offered an effective defence, was rare. In most places, the houses were burned. Cattle and other livestock were rounded up, and there were strong suggestions that they were sold for the personal profit of certain New England merchants closely connected with either Lawrence or Governor Shirley of Massachusetts.[39] The deported Acadians themselves encountered a variety of experiences in the colonies from Massachusetts to Georgia. A relatively friendly reception by fellow-Catholics in Maryland — originally established as a Catholic colony — contrasted with forced labour on southern plantations. In Virginia, a group of over 1000 Acadians was refused admission to the colony, and — those who survived the ravages of an epidemic of smallpox — ultimately spent some seven years in exile in England.[40] In Massachusetts and other northern colonies, deported Acadians were resettled in small groups, although many took the first opportunity to move to find other Acadians or to leave for new destinations.

As years passed the deported Acadians began once again to be masters of their own destiny, as far as circumstances allowed. The substantial number exiled in England, along with many of the 1758 deportees, afterwards lived for a time in France, and attempted with the assistance of the former missionary Le Loutre to set up new communities. The Acadians, however, were not French, other than by language and ancestry. Most eventually left for North American locations, notably Louisiana. There, in the 1780s, they joined with large numbers of other Acadians whose journeys had taken them through the various English colonies or through the French West Indies. The foundation of the Acadian —

or Cajun — community in French-speaking Louisiana was no accidental matter, but was the result of deliberate migration by Acadians seeking out compatriots in that area.[41]

The same can be said of the Acadian return to the Maritimes. By its nature, the return of the Acadians is hard to define through historical sources. Even after Acadians regained in 1764 the legal right to live in Nova Scotia, arrivals were not normally well publicized or documented. The process is better portrayed in literary form, as by the novelist Antonine Maillet, than in purely historical accounts. Yet the presence of some 8400 Acadians in the region by 1800, compared with the 1500 or so who remained in the early 1760s, gives clear evidence of the return movement that had taken place. Certainly the new Acadian communities were not the same as the old. With the Fundy marshlands soon re-allocated to incoming New England settlers, Acadians would now live in new locations. Most of these were coastal and most were not well-favoured for agricultural land.[42] Here and in Louisiana, the expulsion had failed to destroy the essential coherence of Acadian society. What the expulsion had done, however, was to exact a high price: in terms of death and privation, and in terms of the abrupt destruction of the old Bay of Fundy communities.

Yet how had this come about, if not by individual villainy on one side or the other? The order for the expulsion was given by Lawrence and the Nova Scotia council. They acted without direct orders, but the British government never subsequently questioned their action and in fact promoted Lawrence to the full office of governor of Nova Scotia in 1756.[43] Considering that the governor of New France had threatened in 1751 to expel "rebel" Acadians from their lands, and the possibility that force had been used in 1750 by Micmac forces to expel the Beaubassin Acadians from their community, it is reasonable at one level to see the deportation as the crushing of a civilian population between military powers: French, British, and Micmac.

At another level, however, there is more to the explanation than that. There is no escaping the fact that the expulsion as such was initiated and carried out by the British authorities. It is equally a fact that the expulsion was not a long-planned act. As late as June 1755, there was no suggestion of a general deportation. Furthermore, the attitudes — on the part of Lawrence and the council — that led eventually to the expulsion did not represent the only possible British view of the Acadians. Ever since the 1740s there had been two such possible views, not one. Each was based on military calculation. Lawrence believed as had the former governor, Edward Cornwallis, that the Acadians were at least partially a military threat to Great Britain. His other predecessors Mascarene and Hopson, however, had believed that the Acadians' presence was in fact advantageous to Great Britain, both militarily and economically. Militarily, even though a few Acadians would always side with France, the acceptance of their neutrality would prevent the majority from doing so. Economically, the Acadians represented a skilled and prosperous agricultural and fishing population.

Throughout the early 1750s, the British had made efforts to ease the dilemma that was indicated by the existence of these two conflicting views. Their strategy had been to bring in British and Foreign Protestant settlers who, it was hoped, would quietly lay the foundations of a stable Protestant population in Nova Scotia, and thus lessen the importance of the Acadians. By the summer of 1755, this policy was in disarray. The population of Halifax had declined substantially since 1750, and the Foreign Protestants had to be settled in Lunenburg rather than among the Acadians. Even the plan of Lawrence and Shirley to settle New Englanders on the isthmus, in 1755, had miscarried. In this situation, and with a major war beginning, the original dilemma reappeared with new urgency. The response of Lawrence and his council was to deal with the perceived Acadian threat as they deemed best — by expulsion.

Yet on the basis of later events, a strong case can be made that it was the view of Mascarene and Hopson that was the more realistic. Even though many Acadians were defeated in 1755, some thousands of others either escaped to Ile Royale or Ile Saint-Jean, or took refuge in locations remote from Halifax, such as on the Miramichi River. Of these an undetermined but significant number did take up arms and sustained guerrilla warfare for the next three years under the leadership of Boishébert. Also on the basis of later events, the deportation can be regarded as militarily unnecessary. The conquests of Louisbourg in 1758, of Quebec in 1759, and of Montreal in 1760, made the Acadian presence irrelevant to any military consideration, by guaranteeing the British ascendancy. Communities that had taken up to 120 years to build were thus destroyed in the interests of a military strategy which was already questionable when implemented and which ceased to matter at all within five years.

What cannot be questioned is the reality that the expulsion of the Acadians marked a profoundly important turning point in the history of the Maritime region. From an Acadian standpoint this is so obvious as to require little elaboration. The entire pattern of Acadian settlement had been reshaped. In the process, the Acadians had experienced a human tragedy, if not on a scale unprecedented in the region — the depopulation suffered by native peoples in the late sixteenth century had been even more costly in human life — then still on a scale that is hard to comprehend fully. The 1750s also comprised a disastrous decade for the Micmac, who were deprived of their most powerful allies by the defeat of the French in 1758. They now entered an era of military decline accompanied by social and economic deterioration.

The 1750s also saw the effective beginning of the repopulation of the region by English-speaking settlers, and by other British-sponsored nationalities. It is true, of course, that there had been some British settlement at Annapolis Royal since the establishment of the military garrison there in 1710. It is also true that the foundation of Halifax had been in 1749. Yet it was during the 1750s that Halifax — despite fluctuations in population in the early part of the decade — established its strong roots as a military, political, and economic centre. It was during the 1750s that the Foreign Protestants' settlement at Lunenburg was established, and by the end of the decade attained considerable economic prosperity and social stability.

Furthermore, it was the decade of the 1750s that saw the foundations laid for the large immigration of New England "planters" that would take place primarily in the years 1760-63. Despite strong suggestions in older historical accounts that the expulsion of the Acadians was carried out specifically so that New England settlers could take their lands, recent scholarship has convincingly questioned the existence of this causal relationship. While Lawrence and Shirley were certainly thinking in terms of New England settlement in a limited area on and to the west of the isthmus, there is no evidence to suggest that a general expulsion was considered by them in advance, let alone that province-wide New England immigration was immediately planned. After 1758, however, circumstances changed.

In general terms, though not in terms of specific planning, the notion of New England settlement was not new in the 1750s. Very soon after the conquest of 1710, hopes had been entertained that settlers from Massachusetts and neighbouring colonies would immigrate in significant numbers.[44] At this time, however, there was still much available land in northern and western New

England, and potential settlers showed no desire to move to the more remote destination of Nova Scotia, especially since there was an existing French-speaking and Roman Catholic population. Also a disincentive was the powerful French military presence on Ile Royale.

These dissuading factors ceased to operate in the 1750s. The expulsion of the Acadians made good land available, at a time when the best New England lands were approaching full settlement. The conquest of Louisbourg offered stability in the sense of freedom from possible French attack. Also in 1758, Nova Scotia came more nearly to resemble the New England colonies in governmental matters, through the opening of the colony's first representative assembly.[45]

The assembly's establishment had not been favoured by Lawrence, who had eventually given in to pressure from London and from Halifax-based New England merchants who hoped to use it for their own political advantage. Nevertheless Lawrence was well aware of the need for new settlement in Nova Scotia and of the fact that New England was the most likely source. In late 1758 he issued a proclamation which invited immigration into the province, and publicized it widely in the New England colonies. In response to questions from potential immigrants, he published a more detailed proclamation in January 1759. The new proclamation promised land grants with no rents payable for the first ten years, government structures similar to those of the New England colonies, military protection from any possible Indian attack, and full religious freedom for all Protestants. This last provision recognized the fact that the immigrants would be largely New England Congregationalists, rather than members of the established Church of England. On the basis of these undertakings, the New England migrations began in 1760, and brought some 5000 settlers to various parts of Nova Scotia by 1763.[46] Also a product of the 1759 proclamation was the scheme of the colonial promoter Alexander McNutt, who brought some hundreds of Ulster settlers to the townships of Truro, Onslow, and Londonderry in 1761 and 1762.[47]

Thus, these major migrations were foreshadowed during the 1750s, even though they would actually take place in the early 1760s. Even before the migrations, a major change had occurred in the population of Nova Scotia, which now comprehended all of today's Maritime region. If we accept Belcher's figure of about 1500 remaining Acadians, and add some 3000 native people, we arrive at a total non-British population of 4500 in Nova Scotia in early 1760. The British population, including for this purpose the Foreign Protestants, stood at approximately 5000. This would encompass some 3000 in Halifax, between 1500 and 2000 at Lunenburg, and a handful of others scattered in other areas. For the first time in this decade, therefore, the majority of the population consisted of British or British-sponsored settlers.[48]

That this was so, and that Acadians were now a small minority in a region where they had started the decade as a clear majority of the population, was owed primarily to the expulsion which had begun in 1755. In part, the events of the decade had been shaped by forces beyond the control of any in Nova Scotia. The competing imperialisms of Great Britain and France comprised the essential background to the deportation of the Acadians. Yet the deportation itself was not inevitable. It depended on a particular interpretation of the military interests of Great Britain: one which was by no means unchallenged even in the Halifax of the early 1750s. That this one view, emphasizing the threat that the Acadians might pose, should have prevailed so strongly in 1755 in the minds of Charles Lawrence and the Nova Scotia council, at the expense of the other interpretation which favoured the continuing Acadian presence, was a major cause of the Acadian disaster. It was also an essential cause of the entire sequence of profound changes which characterized the crucial decade of the 1750s.

NOTES

1. Y.F. Zoltvany, ed., *The French Tradition in America* (New York, 1969), p. 128.
2. Frontenac to King Louis XIV, 6 November 1679, France, Archives des Colonies, C11A, 5, folio 16.
3. M. Tibierge, "Memoir on the Present State of the Province of Acadia," 30 June 1697, in J.C. Webster, ed., *Acadia at the End of the Seventeenth Century* (Saint John, N.B., 1934), p. 155.
4. See also Reid, *Acadia, Maine, and New Scotland*, pp. 160-1; and Jean Daigle, "Nos amis les ennemis: relations commerciales de l'Acadie avec le Massachusetts" (Ph.D. thesis; University of Maine, 1975).
5. Naomi Griffiths, *The Acadians: Creation of a People* (Toronto, 1973), pp. 19-37.
6. Andrew Hill Clark, *Acadia: The Geography of Early Nova Scotia to 1760* (Madison, Wisc., 1968), p. 201.
7. Quoted in Clark, *Acadia*, p. 200. Punctuation added.
8. Gisa I. Hynes, "Some Aspects of the Demography of Port Royal, 1650-1755," *Acadiensis*, 3 (Autumn 1973), pp. 3-17. On this era, see also Naomi Griffiths, "The Golden Age: Acadian Life, 1713-1748," *Histoire sociale/Social History*, 17 (1984), pp. 21-34.
9. G.F.G. Stanley, *New France: The Last Phase, 1744-1760* (Toronto, 1968), pp. 1-25. On the fall of Louisbourg, see G.A. Rawlyk, *Yankees at Louisbourg* (Orono, Maine, 1967).
10. Poem in the *Boston Weekly News-Letter*, 11 May 1749, quoted in Rawlyk, *Yankees at Louisbourg*, p. 159.
11. See the memorandum of Jonathan Belcher, 28 July 1755, in Zoltvany, *French Tradition in America*, pp. 170-5.
12. Paul Mascarene to [Ladeveze], [1752], Journal and Letterbook of Mascarene, Public Archives of Nova Scotia, RG1, Vol. 9, f. 16, p. 330. For a full assessment of Mascarene's Nova Scotia career, see Barry M. Moody, "'A Just and Disinterested Man': The Nova Scotia Career of Paul Mascarene, 1710-1752" (Ph.D. thesis; Queen's University, 1976).

13. Stanley, *New France*, pp. 58-72.
14. See Gérard Finn, "Jean-Louis Le Loutre," DCB, IV, 455.
15. D.C. Harvey, *The French Régime in Prince Edward Island* (New Haven, Connecticut, 1926), p. 169.
16. Order of the Marquis de La Jonquière, 12 April 1751, in N.E.S. Griffiths, ed., *The Acadian Deportation: Deliberate Perfidy or Cruel Necessity?* (Toronto, 1979), p. 83.
17. J. Murray Beck, "Edward Cornwallis," DCB, IV, 170.
18. *Ibid.*, p. 169; W.S. MacNutt, *The Atlantic Provinces: The Emergence of Colonial Society* (Toronto, 1965), p. 54.
19. Quoted in L.F.S. Upton, *Micmacs and Colonists: Indian-White Relations in the Maritime Provinces, 1713-1867* (Vancouver, 1979), p. 41.
20. MacNutt, *Atlantic Provinces*, pp. 55-6; Upton, *Micmacs and Colonists*, p. 57.
21. R.O. MacFarlane, "British Indian Policy in Nova Scotia to 1760," in H.F. McGee, Jr., ed., *The Native Peoples of Atlantic Canada: A History of Indian-European Relations* (Ottawa, 1983), pp. 56-7.
22. Stanley, *New France*, p. 108.
23. Charles Lawrence to Robert Monckton, 30 January 1755, in Griffiths, *Acadian Deportation*, p. 108.
24. Stanley, *New France*, pp. 108-17; I.K. Steele, "Robert Monckton," DCB, IV, 540-1.
25. Phyllis E. LeBlanc, "Charles Deschamps de Boishébert et de Raffetot," DCB, IV, 212-15.
26. Dominick Graham, "Charles Lawrence," DCB, III, 362-3.
27. Hopson to the Lords of Trade, 23 July 1753, in Griffiths, *Acadian Deportation*, pp. 84-5.
28. John Clarence Webster, *The Forts of Chignecto: A Study of the Eighteenth Century Conflict Between France and Great Britain in Acadia* (Shediac, N.B., 1930), pp. 34-5.
29. Petition of Minas Inhabitants, 10 June 1755, in Griffiths, *Acadian Deportation*, pp. 118-19.
30. C.J. d'Entremont, "Joseph Brossard," DCB, III, 87-8; Bernard Pothier, "Louis Du Pont du Chambon de Vergor," DCB, IV, 249-51; Stanley, *New France*, pp. 111-18.
31. Nova Scotia Council Records, 3 July 1755, in Griffiths, *Acadian Deportation*, p. 123.
32. Memorandum of Belcher, 28 July 1755, in Zoltvany, *French Tradition in America*, pp. 170-5.
33. Naomi Griffiths, "The Acadians," DCB, IV, xxvii.
34. Clark, *Acadia*, pp. 344-51.
35. See Finn, "Jean-Louis Le Loutre," DCB, IV, 453-8; Graham, "Charles Lawrence," DCB, III, 361-6.
36. Griffiths, "The Acadians," DCB, IV, xxvii.
37. Barry M. Moody, "John Winslow," DCB, IV, 774-5.
38. Quoted in Naomi Griffiths, *The Acadians: Creation of a People* (Toronto, 1973), p. 58.

39. Stanley, *New France*, pp. 121-2; James C. Hippen, "Thomas Saul," DCB, III, 585-6. On Boishébert at Memramcook, see LeBlanc, "Deschamps de Boishébert," DCB, IV, 213-14.
40. Naomi Griffiths, "Acadians in Exile: The Experiences of Acadians in the British Seaports," *Acadiensis*, 4 (Autumn 1974), pp. 67-84.
41. See Carl A. Brasseaux, "A New Acadia: The Acadian Migrations to South Louisiana, 1764-1802," *Acadiensis*, 15 (Autumn 1985), pp. 123-32.
42. Robert G. LeBlanc, "The Acadian Migrations," *Canadian Geographical Journal*, 81 (1970-1), No. 1, pp. 17-8.
43. Graham, "Charles Lawrence," DCB, III, 364.
44. Clark, *Acadia*, p. 195.
45. George A. Rawlyk, *Nova Scotia's Massachusetts: A Study of Massachusetts-Nova Scotia Relations, 1630-1784* (Montreal, 1973), pp. 217-18.
46. *Ibid.*, pp. 218-21.
47. Phyllis R. Blakeley, "Alexander McNutt," DCB, V, 554-5.
48. See Clark, *Acadia*, pp. 351-2.

FURTHER
READING

In the entire history of the Maritime provinces, the expulsion of the Acadians is probably the event — or series of events — that has attracted the greatest concentration of historical writing. Much of the literature is now quite old, and seems to the modern reader to be unduly biased one way or the other. The accounts given, for example, in James Hannay's *History of Acadia* (J. and A. McMillan, Saint John, N.B., 1879) and in Emile Lauvrière's *La tragédie d'un peuple: histoire du peuple acadien de ses origines à nos jours* (2 vols.; Bossard, Paris, 1922) are both worth reading, but Hannay's harsh judgement of Jean-Louis Le Loutre is no more or less convincing than Lauvrière's similar verdict on Charles Lawrence. Good counterweights to both can be found in the important reassessments of Le Loutre and Lawrence in the *Dictionary of Canadian Biography*, by respectively Gérard Finn (DCB, IV, 453-8) and Dominick Graham (DCB, III, 361-6).

More generally, a good starting-point for any study of Acadian history at this time is with the works of Naomi Griffiths. As well as an anthology of previous writing on the subject in Griffiths, ed., *The Acadian Deportation: Deliberate Perfidy or Cruel Necessity?* (Copp Clark, Toronto, 1969), this author has written two rewarding general studies of the Acadian experience — *The Acadians: Creation of a People* (McGraw-Hill Ryerson, Toronto, 1973), and "The Acadians" (DCB, IV, xvii-xxxi) — in addition to more specialized studies in scholarly journals. See, for example, her "Acadians in Exile: The Experiences of Acadians in the British Seaports," *Acadiensis*, 4 (Autumn 1974), pp. 67-84, and "The Golden Age: Acadian Life, 1713-1748" *Histoire sociale/Social History*, 17 (1984), pp. 21-34.

Other important English-language works on Acadian history of this era include Andrew Hill Clark, *Acadia: The Geography of Early Nova Scotia to 1760* (University of Wisconsin Press, Madison, 1968), and Gisa I. Hynes, "Some Aspects of the Demography of Port Royal, 1650-1755," *Acadiensis*, 3 (Autumn 1973), pp. 3-17. On the related matter of the character of the British administration at Annapolis Royal, see Barry M. Moody, "'A Just and Disinterested Man': The Nova Scotia Career of Paul Mascarene, 1710-1752" (Ph.D. thesis: Queen's University, 1976). Standard works on the French regime on Ile Royale and Ile Saint-Jean remain J.S. MacLennan, *Louisbourg from its Foundation to its Fall, 1713-1758* (Macmillan, London, 1918), and D. C. Harvey, *The French Régime in Prince Edward Island* (Yale University Press, New Haven, Conn., 1926); worth reading too is J.-Henri Blanchard, *The Acadians of Prince Edward Island, 1720-1964* (Le Droit and Leclerc, Ottawa, 1964). There are also a number of more specialized works on aspects of the history of Louisbourg, as well as Christopher Moore's prize-winning *Louisbourg Portraits: Life in an Eighteenth-Century Garrison Town* (Macmillan, Toronto, 1982).

On the narrative and military history of the 1750s, G.F.G. Stanley's *New France: The Last Phase, 1744-1760* (McClelland and Stewart, Toronto, 1969) is a reliable modern account. The expulsion itself, and the Acadians' subsequent experiences, are treated not only in the works of Stanley and Griffiths, but also in other recent studies including the following: Jean Daigle, ed., *The Acadians of the Maritimes: Thematic Studies* (Centre d'études acadiennes, Moncton, 1982); Robert G. LeBlanc, "The Acadian Migrations," *Canadian Geographical Journal*, 81 (1970-71), No. 1, pp. 10-19; and Carl A. Brasseaux, "A New Acadia: The Acadian Migrations to South Louisiana, 1764-1803," *Acadiensis*, 15 (Autumn 1985), pp. 123-32. Also especially relevant to an understanding of the subject are two fictional works which offer contrasting images of the deported Acadians: Antonine Maillet's prize-winning novel, *Pélagie-la-Charrette* (Leméac, Montreal, 1979), and Henry Wadsworth Longfellow's poem *Evangeline* (Tickner, Boston, 1847). For perspective on *Evangeline*, see Naomi Griffiths, "Longfellow's *Evangeline*: The Birth and Acceptance of a Legend," *Acadiensis*, 11 (Spring 1982), pp. 28-41.

The best general account of the Indian experience during the 1750s is in L.F.S. Upton, *Micmacs and Colonists: Indian-White Relations in the Maritime Provinces, 1713-1867* (University of British Columbia Press, Vancouver, 1979). Also still worth reading is R.D. MacFarlane, "British Indian Policy in Nova Scotia to 1760," *Canadian Historical Review* 19 (1938), pp. 154-67, reprinted in H.F. McGee, Jr., ed., *The Native Peoples of Atlantic Canada: A History of Indian-European Relations* (Carleton University Press, Ottawa, 1983).

On the crucially important New England influence on the events of the decade, the works of J. B. Brebner remain important reading: *New England's Outpost: Acadia Before the Conquest of Canada* (Columbia University Press, New York, 1927), and *The Neutral Yankees of Nova Scotia* (Columbia University Press, New York, 1937). Also essential is the more modern work by George A. Rawlyk, *Nova Scotia's Massachusetts: A Study of Massachusetts — Nova Scotia Relations, 1630-1784* (McGill-Queen's University Press, Montreal, 1973). Concerned with a slightly earlier time period, but still relevant, is Rawlyk's *Yankees at Louisbourg* (University of Maine Press, Orono, Maine, 1967).

The British and British-sponsored settlements in Nova Scotia during the 1750s are well studied in a number of works, including W.S. MacNutt,

The Atlantic Provinces: The Emergence of Colonial Society, 1712-1857 (McClelland and Stewart, Toronto, 1965); W.P. Bell, *The "Foreign Protestants" and the Settlement of Nova Scotia* (UTP, Toronto, 1961); and Esther Clark Wright, *Planters and Pioneers: Nova Scotia, 1749-1775* (Lancelot Press, Windsor, N.S., 1978). On this topic, as on all other facets of the decade of the 1750s, the relevant biographies in the *Dictionary of Canadian Biography*, volumes III, IV, and V, are also essential reading.

THE 1780s:
DECADE OF MIGRATION

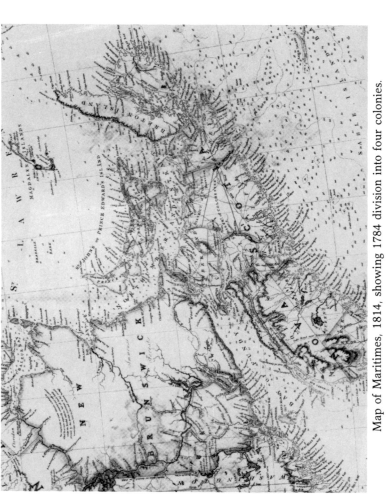

Map of Maritimes, 1814, showing 1784 division into four colonies.

In 1780 North America was again a continent at war. The conflict was even more complex than the wars of the 1740s and 1750s, for although the war of the American Revolution was partly a war between nations — Great Britain opposing the United States and its allies, France and Spain — it was also a civil war within the former Thirteen Colonies. According to one often-cited estimate, about one-third of the British-American colonists initially favoured the revolution, while one-third opposed it, and a further one-third were indifferent. With the total population approaching 2.5 million, that would suggest a figure well over 800,000 for potential adherents of the Loyalist side in the revolutionary war. Not all did become active Loyalists, but a modern estimate has suggested that as many as 384,000 may in fact have become committed to the cause.[1] Many of these Loyalists left the United States as refugees at the end of the war, and a substantial number chose to settle in the Maritime provinces. Their migration, and a series of related migrations by other peoples, had the effect of drastically reshaping the population patterns and the political boundaries of the region. The decade of the 1780s was thus a time of fundamental change.

As the decade opened, the nature of the changes that the revolutionary crisis might bring about was not yet predictable. The outbreak of the war in 1775 had obviously raised the possibility that the revolution would find substantial support in Great Britain's other North American provinces outside of the Thirteen Colonies. Yet this did not come about, or at least not on a scale that promised any effective contribution to the revolutionary cause. Newfoundland, geographically far removed from the mainland colonies and economically tied to Great Britain, was never a likely candidate to join the revolution. The province of Quebec, on the other hand, might have been so considered if its predominantly French-speaking population had not felt more reason to mistrust the British-American colonists than the existing British rulers. As it was, even a partly successful invasion of Quebec by forces of the Continental army in the winter of 1775-76 was insufficient to prompt widespread support for the revolution among the *Canadiens*.[2]

On the Island of St. John, meanwhile — which had gained its autonomy from Nova Scotia in 1769, though not until 1798 adopting its present name of Prince Edward Island — recent British immigrants predominated among the approximately 1500 inhabitants and there was no evidence of any support for the revolution.[3] Although the same could not be said for Nova Scotia, most active support for the revolutionary cause was quickly suppressed or discouraged, so that this colony too came out in support of the British and Loyalist side.

To some extent, as Loyalist refugees were often fond of pointing out in later years, underlying divisions persisted in Nova Scotia. In the early days of the war, there were serious efforts to recruit military support for the revolution, even though successful only on a small scale. Jonathan Eddy, a veteran of the siege of Fort Beauséjour in 1755 and later one of the New England planters on the Isthmus of Chignecto, declared for the revolutionary cause in the summer of 1775. So too did Eddy's friend and Chignecto neighbour, John Allan. That both were members of the Nova Scotia assembly, even though Eddy was about to be disqualified from the House for non-attendance, gave some credibility to their leadership. Yet an attempt by Eddy to storm Fort Cumberland (the old Fort Beauséjour) in November 1776 was easily repulsed by the fort's British defenders. Eddy had raised only some 180 supporters, including a number of Maliseets and Acadians, as well as Chignecto settlers.[4] Ultimately a more successful pro-revolutionary leader was Ambroise Saint-Aubin, a Maliseet chief who was with Eddy at Fort Cumberland and subsequently maintained contact with the revolutionary armies further south through the intermediacy of John Allan. Even Saint-Aubin, however, was unable to sustain a united front in favour of the revolution. He fled into Maine in 1777 when another Maliseet group under Pierre Tomah began to pursue a policy of selective cooperation with both sides in the war.[5]

The policy of Tomah and his followers involved a form of neutrality. "Neutrality" has also been a term frequently applied to characterize the prevailing attitude of the New England planters in Nova Scotia. "We were almost all of us born in New England," declared a Yarmouth petition in late 1775, in protest against the possibility of call-up for military service. Torn between "natural affection" to families still in New England, and on the other hand the ties of "good Faith and Friendship to our King and Country," the petitioners asked "if we may be permitted at this time to live in a peacable State."[6] The government of Nova Scotia, confronted by similar statements from other planter communities, made some concessions — notably in allowing local militias to stay at home except in the case of an invasion — while predictably refusing to accept the principle of neutrality. It would be simplistic to contend that neutrality was the aim of all Nova Scotia planters. Varied initial tendencies to support one side or the other were complicated not only by the strength of the British military presence in Halifax but also by the competing attractions of a major series of evangelical revivals. As the war went on, it affected Nova Scotians more and more directly, whether in the operations of Halifax as a naval base, in skirmishes with revolutionary privateers around the coast, or in the service of Nova Scotians — as well as Newfoundlanders and St. John Islanders — in loyal regiments such as the Royal Fencible Americans and the Royal Highland Emigrants. Nova Scotia did not join the American Revolution, and its pro-British role in the war was greater than many Loyalist refugees would ever be willing to admit.

Nevertheless, the main battles took place further south. At the start of the war it was entirely possible — even probable — that the revolutionary cause would be defeated. To be sure, the failure of the British and Loyalist forces to take decisive advantage of their early military superiority was followed by a humiliating British surrender at Saratoga Springs in October 1777. Early the next year the revolutionaries successfully negotiated their alliance with France, and in 1779 they gained the support of Spain. Even so, as the 1780s opened the military initiative remained with the other side, as was shown in the British capture of Charleston, South Carolina, in May 1780. Only with the surrender of a large British army to French and American forces at Yorktown, Virginia, in October 1781 did the course of the war decisively change. The independence of the United States was formally recognized by Great Britain in the Treaty of Paris, signed in 1783.[7]

This ending of the war did not imply, on the surface, that large numbers of Loyalists would have to leave the United States. The treaty contained a clause by which the U.S. Congress would recommend to the various States that confiscated Loyalist property be restored to its owners.[8] In reality, every state maintained penalties for Loyalists. In the wake of a bitter war, the Loyalists were easily regarded by the victors as traitors who deserved exile at best. Although precise estimates are impossible to make, as many as 100,000 refugees may have left the United States in the late stages of the war and immediately after the peace treaty. Many went to Great Britain, at least initially, and eventually they were scattered throughout much of the remaining British Empire. About 8,000 settled in the province of Quebec, mainly in its western area — later known as Upper Canada, and later still as the province of Ontario — while some 30,000 to 35,000 came to the Maritime provinces. Given that the existing population of the region did not exceed 20,000, the Loyalists' arrival could not help but have a radical effect.[9]

W ho were these Loyalists? A few simple definitions can be given, for what they are worth. A Loyalist was a person who had opposed the Declaration of Independence. A Loyalist was a person who had chosen the losing side in what was, in the Thirteen Colonies, a civil war. A Loyalist was a person who, for whatever reason, favoured the continuing imperial presence of Great Britain in North America. Yet to move beyond these all-too-wide categorizations, it is important to recognize the sheer diversity of the Loyalists. There could be many reasons for opposing the Declaration of Independence in favour of the imperial connection, ranging from pure political idealism to naked self-interest. As with participants in any civil war, most Loyalists' motivations were mixed. So were those of the revolutionaries, and the two sides mirrored each other in many ways. Neither was any more "American" than the other: the majority of both sides had their personal roots firmly in North America. Loyalists, like revolutionaries, could be male or female, rich or poor, black, white, or native. Neighbour had fought neighbour. Families had been divided by the conflict, as in the case of Benjamin Franklin and his Loyalist son William, and in many other less famous instances. In short, a Loyalist could be anybody who had lived in the pre-revolutionary colonies.

For all that, it is possible to identify certain kinds of people who were more likely than others to become Loyalists. Some British-Americans had a vested interest in the existing imperial connection, whether because they held public office or because they depended on the lucrative trading connections within the

British Empire. Some were convinced that the claims of the revolutionaries to be supporting the cause of freedom were false, and that what the revolution really stood for was a weakening of the legitimate structures of society and politics that could only lead to the "tyranny of the majority." Others whose motives were influenced by this same principle, though they would not necessarily have articulated it as such, were members of religious, cultural, and ethnic minorities who tended to support the Loyalist cause in disproportionately large numbers. These would include Indian peoples, Blacks, Quakers and Catholics in some areas, and recent immigrant groups such as Scottish highlanders in North Carolina. To many members of such minority groups, British rule seemed to offer a better chance of acceptance and toleration than did the rule of the colonial majority.[10]

Among those who arrived as exiles in the Maritime colonies were representatives of all of these specific sources of Loyalism. Yet the migration as a whole was inevitably characterized by a wide diversity. Analysis of the New Brunswick Loyalists, for example, has shown that they included former soldiers from all ranks of the "provincial" regiments which had fought in the war, and also large numbers of refugees who had simply refused to support the revolution when called on to do so. The largest proportion (over 72 percent) came from the middle colonies of New York, New Jersey, Pennsylvania, Maryland, and Delaware, while just over 22 percent originated in New England, and the remainder in the south. Some 90 percent were American-born, and in their social background farming and the skilled trades predominated. The myth that the Loyalists came largely from the upper classes is thus quite unjustified, even though there was an influential minority of representatives of the old colonial elites. The Loyalists who settled in peninsular Nova Scotia represented a similar diversity, except for the presence of a substantial number (perhaps 20 percent) who were not Americans, but disbanded regular soldiers of British or other European origin. Of the balance, a significant proportion came from the south (some 30 percent), about 20 percent from New England, and again the largest group (50 percent) from the middle colonies.[11]

The large population of Loyalists from the middle colonies was no accident, since New York City had been in British and Loyalist possession continuously from 1776 to late 1783, and became the main departure point for those going into exile. The major ports of entry to Nova Scotia were at Shelburne and at the mouth of the St. John River. Shelburne grew suddenly to have a population of almost 9,000.[12] The mouth of the St. John had an even larger number of arrivals — about 14,000 — and was better able to sustain urban growth on the basis of its river-valley hinterland.[13] In fact, though, neither Saint John nor Shelburne retained predominance as a centre of Loyalist settlement. There were other, though lesser, ports of entry such as St. Andrews, St. Stephen, Annapolis Royal and Halifax. Wherever the exiles landed, moreover, they migrated far and wide throughout the region. By 1784, there was hardly an area of the two Maritime provinces that had not felt in some way the influence of this large migration. Whether the influence was welcome to the existing inhabitants, however, was a more complex question.

Loyalist exiles had an important effect on the development of the two islands in the Gulf of St. Lawrence which had until the 1750s represented the remnant of the French colony of Acadia. In the Island of St. John, they were made especially welcome by the governor, Walter Patterson. Only a few hundred Loyalists made their way to the Island: perhaps 380, including families and slaves, by the middle of 1784, of whom almost half were to leave within two years.[14] Patterson's motives in attempting to attract Loyalist settlement were not altruistic. In 1781, he had initiated an auction of lands owned by absentee proprietors who had fallen behind in their rents payable to the crown. The auctions were of doubtful legality. The main purchasers, moreover, were Patterson himself and a number of his close government associates, and the purchases were made not for cash but for claimed arrears of salary. Patterson and his cohorts had thus acquired large areas of land without real expense. Unfortunately for them, a number of the proprietors involved were not prepared to abandon their investment lightly, and a bitter political dispute ensued. For Patterson, the recruitment of Loyalists gave him and his associates the opportunity to grant out portions of these disputed lands to newcomers. He would thereby create a new group of supporters, whose own vested interest dictated that they uphold the legality of the 1781 auction.[15]

Patterson's maneuver was not sufficient to forestall his eventual dismissal from the governorship in 1787. Ironically, the political opponent who did most to bring about this fall was Captain John MacDonald, a resident land proprietor who had spent the war fighting with a Loyalist regiment, the Royal Highland Emigrants (84th Foot). Not all Loyalists were exiles from the Thirteen Colonies. Yet Patterson did succeed in implicating

Governor Walter Patterson

Loyalist immigrants in the land dispute, and this was one major factor in ensuring that almost another century would go by before the Prince Edward Island land controversies would be laid to rest. The Loyalist immigration had thus had the effect of entrenching an existing political division, even though in this case the Loyalists themselves had not been the initiators of the episode.[16]

In Cape Breton, the arrival of the Loyalists brought with it division of a different kind, and this time with more active Loyalist participation from the start. Abraham Cuyler was a New York Loyalist who moved to Montreal in 1782. A member of the Loyalist elite — he was a former mayor of Albany, New York — he soon became involved in organizing schemes for settlement of the refugees, and proposed that 3,000 should be directed to Cape Breton. Travelling to London for the winter of 1783-4, Cuyler was successful in persuading the secretary of state, Lord Sydney, that Cape Breton merited the status of an autonomous colony. With a potentially large Loyalist population, and a valuable natural resource in the form of its coalfield, Cape Breton appeared ready to attain prosperity in its own right. The separation of the province from Nova Scotia took place formally in June 1784.[17]

Apart from the establishment of the province of Cape Breton, Cuyler's expectations were never fulfilled. Of his promised 3,000 Loyalists, only 140 actually reached Cape Breton. The others had proved more sceptical of his scheme than Cuyler had expected, and had refused to leave their temporary refuge in Quebec City. Later arrivals brought the Loyalist population in Cape Breton to about 500. The colony was never overwhelmingly Loyalist in its population as there were also about 300 Acadians — chiefly on or near the offshore Ile Madame — and a shifting population of fishermen from Newfoundland and elsewhere. The first governor, J.F.W. Des Barres, brought with him in late 1784 some 129 British settlers. Thus, even before the arrival of large numbers of highland Scots after the turn of the century, the Loyalists did not dominate Cape Breton in terms of numbers. Nor did they get their own way politically, as bitter factional disputes between Cuyler and Des Barres abundantly demonstrated. Furthermore, the autonomy of the island was not long-lived; by 1820 internal political disputes had led the British government to impose reunion with Nova Scotia on an unwilling Cape Breton. In the 1780s, however, Loyalists had not only established a number of prominent island communities, including the new capital, Sydney — named after Lord Sydney — but had also prompted and participated in the establishment of Cape Breton for the time being as a colony in itself.[18]

J. F. W. DesBarres

Cape Breton had become, on 18 June 1784, one of four Maritime colonies. Also split off from Nova Scotia on that day was the Loyalist province *par excellence*, New Brunswick. The New Brunswick Loyalist immigrants numbered about 14,500. The previous population of the territory now to be known as New Brunswick numbered only some 4,000 at most: about 1,600 Acadians, 1,400 English-speaking "pre-Loyalist" settlers, and up to 1,000 Maliseet, Micmac, and Passamaquoddy. Thus, the Loyalists comprised a substantial majority in the province.[19]

There had been more than one scheme for a new province in this territory. As early as 1779 the British government had pondered the notion of establishing a Loyalist province here if the war should go badly, and the result had been a detailed proposal drawn up by William Knox, the undersecretary of state for the colonies. Knox's recommendation was for a colony to be known as New Ireland. The proposal was never put into practice, although it did have an influence on the eventual partition of 1784.[20] The partition was also heavily influenced, however, by the intervention of a determined and coherent group of Loyalist leaders.

From the beginning, the Loyalist leaders in Nova Scotia had an uneasy relationship with the government and the existing population of their adopted province. Central to the attitudes of articulate and formerly wealthy Loyalists was the fact that they had sacrificed their possessions and the personal safety of themselves and their families for the noble cause of the unity of the British Empire. Even if in reality their motivations may not always have been as pure as that, the reality of their sufferings gave their claim strong moral force. When they looked at Nova Scotia, they saw a province made up of people whose war record was more questionable. Certainly there had been Nova Scotians — as well as St. John Islanders — who had served in Loyalist regiments.[21] Yet this was offset, in the eyes of the Loyalist refugees, by the attitude of the "Neutral Yankees." Furthermore, the town of Halifax had profited handsomely from the war, through naval expenditures as well as from the successful ventures of privateers. Wealthy Haligonians had not had to sacrifice their own interests in the imperial cause. On the contrary, they had enriched themselves. Many of them also enjoyed political power and influence in the clique surrounding Governor John Parr, a retired officer of the British army who had been appointed to his office only in 1782 and was still acclimatizing himself to it. For Loyalists to be governed, as they saw it, by war profiteers, was unjust and degrading.[22]

To make matters worse, the government of Nova Scotia was overwhelmed by the logistical and bureaucratic problems raised by the arrival of the Loyalists. To provide basic food and shelter for the thousands of refugees was difficult enough. Even more complex was the task of dealing with Loyalist demands for land grants. The status of Loyalist entitled a person to claim compensation for losses brought about by the revolution, as well as a military pension if the individual had served in the war. These payments were not the responsibility of the provincial government. The allocation of land, however, necessarily was so. The number of claims involved, the lack of an adequate number of surveyors, and a cumbersome administrative structure combined to cause serious delays. Loyalists even competed among themselves in submitting claims. The "Committee of 55," for example, consisted of a number of well-to-do New York Loyalists who, in the summer of 1783, claimed grants of 5000 acres each in peninsular Nova Scotia: their petition served only to bring forth a counterpetition from 600 other Loyalist refugees condemning the greed of the original petitioners.[23]

One obvious way out of the chaos, which many Loyalists were inclined to blame on Parr and his associates, was to press ahead with plans for a new province. In the winter of 1783-84, members of the Loyalist elite waged an effective political campaign directed at achieving this goal. The leader in Nova Scotia itself was Edward Winslow, who worked closely with a London-based fellow-Massachusetts Loyalist, Ward Chipman. Chipman in turn endeavoured to raise support among other Loyalists in London, and in the government, through such contacts as William Knox. Plans for Saint John to be made the administrative centre of all British North America were rejected by the government; but Winslow, Chipman, and their colleagues had their reward in the creation of New Brunswick. "Yes — by God!," Winslow proclaimed, "we will be the envy of the American states."[24]

Whether that prophecy would be fulfilled was yet to be seen. For the province of Nova Scotia, however, there was more immediate cause for envy. Nova Scotia had abruptly been deprived of large areas of territory, even including much of the Isthmus of Chignecto. The line had been drawn at the Missaguash River, between the sites of the former rival forts of the French and British. Thus the prosperous agricultural settlement of Sackville was outside the boundaries of Nova Scotia. At a more basic level of self-interest, no fees could now be charged by Nova Scotia officials for land grants made out to New Brunswick Loyalists.

For Parr the division of the province must have brought some relief from the complex and disagreeable business of Loyalist resettlement. Yet it also implied a significant diminution in the extent and the importance of Nova Scotia.[25]

Not that Nova Scotia was even now bereft of Loyalist refugees. In fact the population of Loyalists and disbanded soldiers in Nova Scotia was probably larger than in New Brunswick. Because of the chaotic circumstances accurate numbers are difficult to establish, but estimates for Nova Scotia range up to 20,000.[26] Shelburne, as the port of arrival for many of these, retained a large population for a few years. By the end of the decade, however, two-thirds of the houses in the town were deserted.[27] Shelburne provided a revealing example of the disappointment of Loyalist expectations. Originally selected by Loyalist groups as a fine harbour surrounded by potential agricultural land, the intention for Shelburne was that it would become a major trading port. Its commerce would be enhanced by timber production and fisheries, while the fabric of the community would be strengthened by agriculture. The reality was quite different. The land was stony, the town site too far from the open sea to be ideal as a fishing centre, and there was little timber readily accessible. Delays in the granting of land, and the failure to attract interest in Shelburne as a potential naval base, combined with these environmental factors to frustrate the development of the town.[28]

The long-term result was depopulation, before Shelburne finally found its stability as a much smaller community. The short-term result was serious conflict among the Loyalists. Frictions developed as blame for the town's difficulties was allocated and reallocated. Disputes over land distribution became class conflicts, as it became evident that wealthy members of the elite had acquired prime harbourfront lots of up to 500 acres, while others were still waiting for confirmation even of meagre areas of farm land. The government's surveyor for the district, Benjamin Marston, was disturbed by the resentment that prevailed, and declared that "this cursed levelling spirit must be crushed by every means or we shall be for rebellion soon."[29]

Yet when the violence did break out, in late July 1784, it was not a simple case of rebellion. Although anti-government feeling was undoubtedly one element in causing riots in the streets, a further strong element was racial conflict between Loyalists. Among the most important groups of Loyalist migrants were the free Black Loyalists, who numbered about 3500 and thus comprised at least 10 per cent of the migration as a whole.[30] Even

Ward Chipman

General Thomas Carleton

this number did not comprehend all of the Black Loyalists, for there were probably another 2000 who came as slaves; only in later decades was slavery gradually eliminated from the Maritimes. The free Blacks, in most cases, had gained their freedom by rallying to the Loyalist cause, and they had been promised the same entitlements as other Loyalists. Over 1500 were living in the Shelburne district in the summer of 1784.[31]

The experience of these Black Loyalists would soon show that their supposedly equal rights and privileges would not be tolerated by fellow migrants. In a town experiencing serious economic dislocation, with unemployment and underemployment, the Blacks were a conspicuous group. On 26 July 1784, Marston recorded in his diary that "the disbanded soldiers have risen against the Free negroes to drive them out of Town, because they labour cheaper than they — the soldiers." The next day, the riots continued. "The soldiers force the free negroes to quit the Town," Marston wrote, shortly before he himself fled to take refuge in Halifax, "[and have] pulled down about 20 of their houses."[32]

The major area of Black settlement in the Shelburne district would henceforth be not in the town itself, but in nearby Birchtown. There the community attempted to survive by farming largely barren land, and by finding wage labour in the shrinking Shelburne economy. The experience of Black Loyalists in Shelburne was unusually dramatic, in that open violence had been used against them. Essentially, however, the results did not differ from the situations of other Black Loyalist communities, whether in Guysborough County, in Annapolis County, in Halifax or Preston, or in Saint John, New Brunswick. Relegation to lands unwanted by other Loyalists effectively restricted the opportunities open to Blacks, together with explicit restrictions as in the 1785 charter of the city of Saint John which opened the freedom of the city — necessary for practising a trade, or selling any goods within city limits — only to "American and European White inhabitants."[33]

The rise and decline of Shelburne, therefore, gave clear evidence of the high hopes and the disappointments that often accompanied Loyalist settlement. The dispersal of many of the early Shelburne inhabitants contributed, along with the settlement and migration of those who had arrived at other Nova Scotia ports, to the diffusion of the Loyalists throughout the province. Some disillusioned refugees quietly made their way back to their former homes in the United States, and this process continued throughout the 1780s.[34] The majority, however, became permanent residents

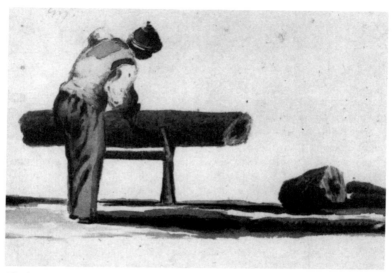

Black woodcutter at Shelburne, 1788. Watercolour by William Booth

of communities up and down the Atlantic coast from Guysborough south-westward and around to Yarmouth and Digby, of the Annapolis Valley and King's County, of Truro and along the shore to Parrsboro, of other Cumberland communities and eastward through Pictou and Antigonish. In short, their settlement and their influence pervaded the province.[35]

The migration of Loyalists thus had important direct results for the Maritime region. The sheer numbers of the new immigrants ensured their influence in New Brunswick and Nova Scotia, and in Cape Breton and the Island of St. John they were influential also, though in ways that reflected their smaller numbers in these provinces. The direct results, however, were not the only important ones. Also crucial in this decade of migration were the indirect results brought about through interactions with the previously established peoples of the region. In the two provinces of large-scale Loyalist settlement, different patterns emerged.

Relations between Loyalist immigrants and existing populations in Nova Scotia were often initially hostile. Loyalist contempt for the provincial government and the Halifax elite was strong from the start. Governor Parr in turn was sceptical of the Loyalist claims to have suffered mightily for a noble cause. "I have to be sure," Parr confided to a correspondent in September 1784, "a most troublesome, discontented, disappointed, over expecting Race of Mortals to deal with. . . . "[36] For some years after, Parr was drawn into the position of referee in disputes between Loyalists and pre-Loyalists that arose from successful Loyalist efforts in the 1785 elections for the provincial assembly. Loyalist members launched frequent attacks against government officials, and the resulting series of political and constitutional disputes came to an end only after Parr's death in 1791 and his succession as governor by a Loyalist, and pre-revolutionary governor of New Hampshire, John Wentworth.[37]

Political disputes reflected resentment between Loyalists and pre-Loyalists at the local level. The arrival of articulate and politically active Loyalists presented a seeming threat to existing local elites, while the overall numbers of the immigrants raised fears of competition for land and employment as well as for public office. Nevertheless, these suspicions proved able to be allayed as time went by. In part, the diversity of the Loyalists contributed to reconciliation. The Loyalists included people of many different ethnic groups, religious denominations, and social class backgrounds. Affinities in any of these areas could readily offset the distinction between Loyalist and pre-Loyalist. Thus, apart from early quarrels, the results of Loyalist immigration confirmed, in certain important respects, political and social patterns that already existed. Politically, Loyalist leaders soon discovered that their hostility to the Halifax elite was shared by many pre-Loyalists outside of the capital. By strengthening the opposition to the domination of Halifax, the Loyalists contributed to the development of urban-rural tension as a major element of Nova Scotia's political culture.[38]

Also in the area of ethnic relations, the Loyalists could reinforce existing trends. The major example is in the influx of Scottish Highlanders as veterans of Loyalist regiments such as the Royal Highland Emigrants. While some of these disbanded soldiers had been recruited in Nova Scotia itself, or on the Island of St. John — Highland settlement on the Island dated from 1770, and from 1773 in Nova Scotia — many came from elsewhere. Whether enlisted in North Carolina, pressed into service directly on arrival in Boston or New York from Scotland, or otherwise recruited, many Highland newcomers came to Nova Scotia among the Loyalist immigrants. The development of the important Highland presence in Nova Scotia, interrupted by the revolutionary war, was thus resumed and would continue with further large direct immigrations from Scotland in future years.[39] On a smaller scale the same can be said for the Irish. Although there had been Irish settlers in Halifax from its founding, and Scotch-Irish Presbyterians in the Truro area from 1761, the numbers were still small by the 1780s and large increases would come only after the turn of the century. Nevertheless there were Irish Loyalists, even though exact numbers are hard to determine. The year 1786, for example, saw the foundation of the Charitable Irish Society in Halifax, with a former officer of the Royal Highland Emigrants, Gerald Fitzgerald, as its first secretary, and with at least ten Loyalist refugees among the others of the 88 charter members.[40]

In these respects, the Loyalists reinforced existing political and social tendencies in Nova Scotia. It is noteworthy, however, that certain of the peoples of the province were excluded from these convergences. Acadian communities, separated by language and in most cases by geographic isolation, had limited contact with Nova Scotia Loyalists. Micmac bands in various parts of the province did have contact with them, usually with the result that Loyalist settlers brought about the removal of Indian people to reserve land. The Micmac had declined as a military force after the defeat of France in the 1750s and one contemporary observer noted in 1787 that "their weakness, added to their prudence, will certainly prevent them from making any disturbances."[41] The decade of the 1780s was one of migration for native people in Nova Scotia: of migration to small and often isolated reserves. Also isolated were the various branches of one important Loyalist group already mentioned, the Black Loyalists. That the Black communities around the province had become marginal to neighbouring settlements, with detrimental social and economic results, was reflected in the later migration of some 1200 Black Loyalists to West Africa, where they founded the town of Freetown in the colony of Sierra Leone. Although this migration took place in 1792, it belongs in a real sense to the 1780s for it represents the exclusion of the Black Loyalists from equal participation in the benefits that all Loyalists were supposedly to have enjoyed in that decade.[42]

In a general sense, the influence of the Loyalists in Nova Scotia was in proportion to their share of the population. Loyalist immigrants to the province numbered about the same as the existing population, or only slightly more. Considering also the strong position of the Halifax elite, and also to some extent of local elites elsewhere, there was no likelihood that Nova Scotia would be overwhelmed. Instead the Loyalists tended to reinforce existing patterns, whether of rural-urban conflict or of Celtic immigration. Insofar as the marginalization of certain social groups was also an existing trend, it too was carried forward. Nova Scotia after the Loyalist migration was a society characterized by greater diversities than before, but also by more entrenched divisions.

The New Brunswick experience was different, because of the much larger Loyalist proportion of the overall population. For New Brunswick, the 1780s comprised a decade of migration indeed, for in this province the Loyalist immigration brought about wholesale displacements of existing populations. Native people were among the first to be affected. The Passamaquoddy, for example, saw a large area of their traditional land allocated to Loyalists founding the town of St. Andrews and neighboring settlements. In close contact with John Allan, who had spent the later years of the war as commander of revolutionary forces northeast of the Penobscot River (in Maine), the main part of the Passamaquoddy people now moved southward. They settled first on Indian Island, in Passamaquoddy Bay, and ultimately on the mainland, in today's Washington County, Maine.[43]

The Maliseet of the St. John Valley also experienced pressures on their land as a result of the Loyalist migration, especially after the establishment of the new provincial capital of Fredericton. The major Maliseet centre since the middle part of the century was at Aukpaque, a short distance upriver from Fredericton. Although it was not until 1794 that this site was actually given over to a Loyalist settler, tensions between Loyalist and Maliseet had existed from the start. In the spring of 1786, Fredericton came briefly under the pressure of having a large number of potentially hostile Maliseet encamped near the town, during the trial of two Loyalist settlers for the murder of a native man whose dog they had accused of killing farm animals. The Maliseet had the satisfaction of seeing the two convicted, and yet this one redress of a specific grievance could not forestall the loss of lands that would soon prompt their removal to reserve lands at Kingsclear and elsewhere in the upper part of the valley.[44] Similar problems were experienced by the Micmac in areas further north in the province, especially on the Miramichi and Richibucto rivers. In 1788, for example, Governor Thomas Carleton issued a proclamation excluding Indian people from living within the limits — as yet ill-defined — of the village of Richibucto. By the turn of the century, one historian has observed, "the Indian reservation had become an accepted feature of New Brunswick life."[45] This was partly the result of the military decline of native peoples, but the direct cause was the taking over of Indian lands by Loyalists well armed with their land titles.

The Acadians of the St. John Valley were also displaced. In most cases they, like native people, held no formal land title. Nevertheless, Acadian settlement in the area was long-established. Even before the expulsion the population had been growing, especially at St. Anne's Point, on the present site of Fredericton. At the time of the expulsion, several hundred refugees made their way upriver, and despite military harassment in the late 1750s the numbers remained substantial. At the time of the Loyalists' arrival, some 350 Acadians were living just upstream from the original site of St. Anne's Point, which had been burned in 1759 by New England troops. The immediate result of the Loyalist arrival, and specifically of disbanded soldiers from Loyalist regiments, was the forced eviction of a number of Acadians from the lands they occupied. By early 1786, dispossessed Acadians were petitioning Governor Carleton for relief of their "most deplorable condition," and even the Loyalist leader Edward Winslow agreed that they had been "most unjustly ousted of their land."[46]

Ultimately, the matter was settled by a process of negotiation. Both Winslow and Carleton were willing to agree that some form of redress should be offered to displaced Acadians, but they were also necessarily committed to Loyalist settlement of the area. A possible solution was proposed by Louis Mercure, a young Acadian — though not from the old-established Nova Scotia communities — who had been born on Ile Saint-Jean shortly before the expulsion. During the revolutionary war he and his brother Michel had been military couriers for the British, and enjoyed some prestige and influence with government authorities as a result. As early as in 1785 Louis Mercure petitioned for land to be set aside for Acadian settlement in the Madawaska region, far up the St. John Valley. The approval of the provincial government was quickly given, and the Mercures led the first Acadian migration to that area. Settlers were eventually drawn not only from the Fredericton district, but also from the Kennebecasis valley, nearer to Saint John, where Acadians had also been displaced. The movement now quickly assumed the character of a voluntary rather than a forced migration. Settlers arrived not only from elsewhere in New Brunswick but also from the province of Quebec, both Acadians and Canadians. The establishment of the Madawaska community, destined along with the north shore of the province and the Moncton-Shediac area of the southeast to emerge as one of the three main Acadian areas of the province, thus offered a solution to Acadian-Loyalist tensions in the St. John Valley. Nevertheless it was a solution to a conflict which had showed once again the danger posed by the Loyalist migration to the stability of existing populations.[47]

That the Loyalists had the ability to prompt major migrations of older-established inhabitants was due in part to their possession of formal land deeds. Even the pre-Loyalist settlers of Maugerville, many of whom had questionable titles, found themselves liable to damaging conflicts with the newcomers over land.[48] The Loyalists also had their way, however, because of the power of overwhelming numbers. In the province as a whole, Loyalists outnumbered other inhabitants by almost four to one. As well as in land questions, this situation had important results in the formation of the political and social structures of the province.

New Brunswick was founded in a spirit of optimism and idealism. For leading members of the Loyalist elite such as Winslow or Chipman, the province would represent all that the Thirteen Colonies might have been if they had not made the disastrous mistake of breaking with the British Empire. New Brunswick, like the other Maritime provinces, retained the right to trade with such important areas of the Empire as the British West Indies, a right now denied to the United States. A sound basis of popular representation in the elected assembly, balanced by strong powers remaining in the hands of the governor and crown-appointed councils, would ensure that the province would never fall into the kind of anarchy that many Loyalists foresaw for the United States. As Winslow had predicted, so his Loyalist colleagues believed: that New Brunswick would soon be envied by the unfortunate inhabitants of the United States.

The late 1780s gave apparent evidence that the United States was indeed in serious trouble. A brief armed rebellion led by Daniel Shays in rural Massachusetts in 1786-87 was easily interpreted as a sign of worse things to come. The truth was, however, that New Brunswick too was a society deeply divided. Unlike the situation in Nova Scotia, where the large existing population had already established social and political patterns which were modified but not erased by the Loyalists, in New Brunswick it was the internecine quarrels of the Loyalists themselves which soon became institutionalized in the political culture of the province.

First Government House, Fredericton

The idealism of the Loyalist elite in New Brunswick, while undoubtedly sincere, was accompanied in a number of prominent individuals by a large appetite for personal wealth and power. Through large engrossments of land, and well-paid public offices, such leaders could attempt to build their fortunes once again to the levels they had enjoyed before the revolution. They did not always succeed. Winslow, for example, was the most assiduous office-seeker of all, and enjoyed a series of high public appointments which eventually included a judgeship in the provincial supreme court, even though he was not a lawyer. Yet he died still enmeshed in debts dating from the time of the revolution.[49] Be that as it might, the seeming enrichment of the elite was inevitably offensive to Loyalists who believed that they had sacrificed just as much to the loyal cause, but who were not admitted to the spoils of office and extensive land ownership.

Furthermore, the idealism of the leaders carried its own dangers. All too easily, a profound belief in the direction being taken by the province under the influence of the elite, and of their sympathetic ally Governor Thomas Carleton, could lapse into intolerance of any opposition. For those who considered the building of a loyal and well-ordered society in New Brunswick to be a sacred trust, political opposition amounted to nothing less than disloyalty and factionalism.

Thus, although the first provincial election in 1785 yielded an assembly dominated overwhelmingly by Loyalists, it contained the nucleus of an opposition to the elite in the person of Elias Hardy. Hardy, elected in Northumberland county, was himself a Loyalist but had already emerged as a leading critic of wealth and privilege. He had written, for example, the counter-petition which had frustrated the efforts of the "Committee of 55" to secure large personal land grants.[50] During the election campaign, moreover, bitter disputes had broken out in Saint John between government candidates, known because of the area where they lived as "Upper Covers," and the "Lower Covers" or opposition candidates. Both sides were Loyalists. The Lower Covers, however, had been excluded from land grants in the most desirable area of the city, and from public office; they also tended to be lower on the social scale, and had their origins more often in New York and New Jersey than in the case of the more largely New England background of the Upper Covers. The Upper Covers prevailed, but only amidst electoral violence, and questionable disallowances of Lower Cove votes. It was a costly victory, for what it most aptly showed was the depth of division within Loyalist ranks.[51]

In New Brunswick political life of the 1780s, the stakes were high. They were high because the province was overwhelmingly populated by new arrivals who had their fortunes to make or to restore, whether on a large or small scale. Among those who looked to public office and large land ownership to accomplish this, there was inevitably competition, and especially the bitter conflict of successful and unsuccessful aspirants. The depth of emotion was made all the greater by the underlying sense of grievance of Loyalist refugees who saw themselves as sufferers in a high cause, and thus morally entitled to a just reward. For those who succeeded in attaining wealth and office, it seemed no more than their due. For those who did not, feelings of aggrievement ran deep. It was parodoxical that the attempt to build a united and well-ordered society should have led to deep-seated disputes that were both political and social in origin. Yet given the large numbers of the Loyalists, the diversity of their origins, and the urgency of their needs, it was not surprising that their divisions would quickly emerge as the sources of major conflicts in the province.

The 1780s comprised a decade of migration. Central to the experience of the Maritime region at this time was the large and diverse immigration of Loyalists, including civilian Loyalists, disbanded provincial troops, and a smaller representation of British and foreign disbanded regular soldiers. Also important was the series of secondary migrations, of Acadians and native people within the region and of Black Loyalists to Africa, that directly or indirectly resulted from the Loyalist influx. The entire pattern of settlement of the four Maritime provinces was rearranged.

The legacy of the Loyalists was as diverse as they themselves were. In many areas of the provinces they were the founders of new communities. Shelburne, Guysborough, Saint John, Fredericton, Sydney: these are only a few examples. Loyalist immigrants helped to redraw the political map by altering provincial boundaries with the creation of the provinces of New Brunswick and Cape Breton. They also left a cultural legacy as represented, for example, in the foundation in the 1780s of the two King's Colleges, at Windsor and Fredericton. In a more general cultural sense their arrival ensured that the region would have strong affinities, not only with Great Britain, but also with the United States from whence they came, while also contributing to the diversity of ethnic cultures.

The Loyalist migration thus had enduring results, reinforcing the claim that this decade was a crucial formative era for the Maritimes and giving substance to the sense of pride with which the Loyalist heritage has so often been regarded, especially in New Brunswick. Yet in some important respects the establishment of the Loyalists was dearly bought. Native and Acadian populations paid a disproportionate share of the price in the form of dislodgement from their existing lands. So, to some extent, did other pre-Loyalist settlers. And not all Loyalists shared equally in the benefits, as the Black experience eloquently attested.

Most paradoxically of all, for a group whose members were entitled after 1789 to add the letter "U.E." to their names, representing the principle of Unity of the Empire, the Loyalists brought dispute and division wherever they went. As well as specific local conflicts with previously-established inhabitants, they deepened existing socio-political divisions in Nova Scotia and the Island of Saint John, and started their own in New Brunswick and Cape Breton. In the wake of their strenuous but unsuccessful efforts to preserve the unity of the empire, the Loyalists thus spread discord in their adopted provinces.

This conflict can be explained at least in part by the simple fact that the Loyalist migration made the population of the region larger and more diverse than ever before in its human history. The population was larger now than even in the era prior to

European contact at the turn of the sixteenth century. Size and diversity implied complexity, and complexity in turn implied a society in which internal conflicts would inevitably arise.

That these changes would take place in the course of the decade could not have been predicted in 1780. The outcome of the war was still in doubt at that time, and even success for the revolution was not bound to result in the kind of migrations that eventually did take place. By 1783, however, it had become clear that developments were under way that would permanently change the face of the Maritime provinces. Once again, in the crucial decade of the 1780s, strong outside forces combined with events within the region itself to produce a major historical turning-point.

NOTES

1. Wallace Brown, *The King's Friends: The Composition and Motives of the American Loyalist Claiments* (Providence, R.I., 1965), pp. 249-51.
2. Hilda Neatby, *Quebec: The Revolutionary Age, 1760-1791* (Toronto, 1966), pp. 146-53; C. Grant Head, *Eighteenth-Century Newfoundland: A Geographer's Perspective* (Toronto, 1976), pp. 196-202.
3. J.M. Bumsted, "The Patterson Regime and the Impact of the American Revolution on the Island of St. John, 1775-1786," *Acadiensis*, 13 (Autumn 1983), pp. 47-52.
4. G.A. Rawlyk, "Jonathan Eddy," DCB, V, 295-6.
5. Alice R. Stewart, "John Allan," DCB, V, 15-17; Richard I. Hunt, "Ambroise Saint-Aubin," DCB, IV, 693; Hunt, "Pierre Tomah," DCB, IV, 735-6.
6. Quoted in J.B. Brebner, *The Neutral Yankees of Nova Scotia: A Marginal Colony During the Revolutionary Years* (New York, 1937; reprinted Toronto, 1969), p. 271.
7. On the course of the revolutionary war, see John Richard Allen, *The American Revolution, 1775-1783* (New York, 1954).
8. G.N.D. Evans, ed., *The Loyalists* (Toronto, 1968), p. 31.
9. Wallace Brown and Hereward Senior, *Victorious in Defeat: The Loyalists in Canada* (Toronto, 1984), pp. 31-50.
10. Ann Gorman Condon, "The Foundations of Loyalty," in Robert S. Allen, ed., *The Loyal Americans* (Ottawa, 1983), pp. 2-3.
11. Esther Clark Wright, *The Loyalists of New Brunswick* (Fredericton, N.B., 1955), pp. 151-62; Neil MacKinnon, "The Loyalists: 'A Different People,'" in Douglas F. Campbell, ed., *Banked Fires — The Ethnics of Nova Scotia* (Port Credit, Ont., 1978), p. 75.
12. Marion Robertson, *King's Bounty: A History of Early Shelburne* (Halifax, 1983), p. 79.
13. *Ibid.*, pp. 239-45; D.G. Bell, *Early Loyalist Saint John: The Origin of New Brunswick Politics 1783-1786* (Fredericton, 1983), p. 17.
14. Andrew Hill Clark, *Three Centuries and the Island* (Toronto, 1959), pp. 57-8.

15. See Bumsted, "Patterson Regime," pp. 59-62; Harry Baglole, "Walter Patterson," *DCB*, IV, 608-9.
16. See F.L. Pigot, "John MacDonald of Glenaladale," *DCB*, V, 514-17.
17. R.J. Morgan, "Abraham Cornelius Cuyler," *DCB*, V, 222-3; Morgan, "The Loyalists of Cape Breton," *Dalhousie Review*, 55 (1975-6), pp. 6-7.
18. *Ibid.*, pp. 9-14.
19. Ann Gorman Condon, *The Envy of the American States: The Loyalist Dream for New Brunswick* (Fredericton, N.B., 1984), pp. 73-8, 85.
20. *Ibid.*, pp. 43-4.
21. Robert S. Allen, "The Loyalist Provincial Corps," in Allen, *Loyal Americans*, p. 11.
22. Condon, *Envy of the American States*, pp. 99-100.
23. *Ibid.*, pp. 89-90; Peter Burroughs, "John Parr," *DCB*, IV, 603-5; Neil MacKinnon, *This Unfriendly Soil: The Loyalist Experience in Nova Scotia, 1783-1791* (Kingston and Montreal, 1986), pp. 87-8; W.S. MacNutt, *The Atlantic Provinces: The Emergence of Colonial Society, 1712-1857* (Toronto, 1965), p. 95.
24. Quoted in Ann Gorman Condon, "Edward Winslow," *DCB*, V, 867; see also Condon, *Envy of the American States*, pp. 114-20.
25. MacNutt, *Atlantic Provinces*, pp. 97-8.
26. MacKinnon, "The Loyalists," p. 70; MacKinnon, *This Unfriendly Soil*, pp. 29-32.
27. Robertson, *King's Bounty*, p. 245.
28. *Ibid.*, pp. 241-3.
29. Quoted in Robertson, *King's Bounty*, p. 127.
30. James W. St. G. Walker, *The Black Loyalists: The Search for a Promised Land in Nova Scotia and Sierra Leone, 1783-1870* (New York, 1976), p. 12.
31. Robertson, *King's Bounty*, p. 83.
32. Journal of Benjamin Marston, in W.O. Raymond, ed., "The Founding of Shelburne and Early Miramichi: Marston's Diary," *Collections of the New Brunswick Historical Society*, 3 (1907), p. 265. See also Robertson, *King's Bounty*, p. 128.
33. W.A. Spray, *The Blacks in New Brunswick* (Fredericton, 1972), p. 34.
34. See Neil MacKinnon, "The Changing Attitudes of the Nova Scotian Loyalists Towards the United States, 1783-1791," *Acadiensis* 2 (Spring 1973), pp. 43-54.
35. MacKinnon, "The Loyalists," p. 71.
36. Parr to Evan Nepean, 3 September 1784, quoted in MacKinnon, "The Loyalists," p. 79.
37. Burroughs, "Parr," *DCB*, IV, 604-5.
38. MacKinnon, "The Loyalists," p. 80; MacKinnon, *This Unfriendly Soil*, pp. 99-106.
39. J.M. Bumsted, *The People's Clearance, 1770-1815* (Edinburgh, 1982), pp. 55-67.
40. H.L. Stewart, *The Irish in Nova Scotia* (Kentville, N.S., [1949]), pp. 19-20; Terrence Punch, *Irish Halifax: The Immigrant Generation,*

1815-1859 (Halifax, 1981), pp. 19-20; "The Charter Membership of the Charitable Irish Society," *Nova Scotia Historical Review*, 6 (1986), pp. 11-15.

41. S. Hollingsworth, quoted in Upton, *Micmacs and Colonists*, p. 83.

42. Walker, *Black Loyalists*, pp. 94-144; see also Walker, "Thomas Peters," DCB, IV, 626-8, and Walker, "David George," DCB, V, 340-2.

43. Stewart, "John Allan," DCB, V, 16; Vincent O. Erickson, "Maliseet-Passamaquoddy," in Bruce G. Trigger, ed., *Handbook of North American Indians, Volume 15, Northeast* (Washington, 1978), pp. 124-5.

44. Erickson, "Maliseet-Passamaquoddy," pp. 124-5; W.S. MacNutt, *New Brunswick: A History* (Toronto, 1963), p. 78; L.F.S. Upton, "Pierre Benoit," DCB, IV, 55.

45. Upton, *Micmacs and Colonists*, pp. 99-100.

46. Quoted in W.O. Raymond, "The First Governor of New Brunswick and the Acadians of the River Saint John," *Proceedings and Transactions of the Royal Society of Canada*, 3rd series, 8 (1914), section 2, pp. 432, 435; see also pp. 420-2.

47. *Ibid.*, pp. 436-40; Sheila Andrew, "Louis Mercure" DCB, V, 589-90; on Mercure's wartime service, see Report of Ebenezer Foster, Fyler Dibble, James White, and Gervis Say, [1783], in *Collections of the New Brunswick Historical Society*, I (1894), p. 113. For a different view of this episode, see Béatrice C. Craig, "Early French Migrations to Northern Maine, 1785-1850," *Maine Historical Society Quarterly*, 25 (1985-6), pp. 230-47. On relations between Loyalists and non-English minorities in Nova Scotia, see MacKinnon, *This Unfriendly Soil*, pp. 106-7.

48. Raymond, "First Governor," pp. 426-36.

49. Condon, *Envy of the American States*, pp. 180-4.

50. Ann Gorman Condon, "Elias Hardy," DCB, IV, 327-9.

51. Bell, *Early Loyalist Saint John*, esp. pp. 118-35.

FURTHER
READING

So much has been written about the Loyalist experience of the 1780s that it is difficult to know where to begin. An area which at one time was neglected, but has been extensively examined in recent years, is the matter of the origins of Loyalism in the Thirteen Colonies. A pioneering survey is presented in W.H. Nelson, *The American Tory* (Oxford University Press, Toronto, 1961), while the works of Wallace Brown provide further analysis: Brown, *The King's Friends: The Composition and Motives of the American Loyalist Claimants* (Brown University Press, Providence, R.I., 1965), and *The Good Americans: The Loyalists in the American Revolution* (William Morrow, New York, 1969). Other relevant works are Paul H. Smith, *Loyalists and Redcoats* (University of North Carolina Press, Chapel Hill, 1964); Robert M. Calhoon, *The Loyalists in Revolutionary America, 1760-1781* (Harcourt Brace Jovanovich, New York, 1973); and Janice Potter, *The Liberty We Seek: Loyalist Ideology in Colonial New York and Massachusetts* (Harvard University Press, Cambridge, 1983). An important recent reappraisal of Loyalism can be found in the works of J.M. Bumsted: "Loyalists and Nationalists: An Essay on the Problem of Definition," *Canadian Review of Studies in Nationalism*, 6 (1979), pp. 218-32; and *Understanding the Loyalists* (Mount Allison University, Sackville, N.B., 1986).

On pre-revolutionary Nova Scotia and its response to the revolution, still worth reading is J.B. Brebner, *The Neutral Yankees of Nova Scotia* (Columbia University Press, New York, 1937). More modern treatments can be found in G.A. Rawlyk, *Nova Scotia's Massachusetts: A Study of Massachusetts — Nova Scotia Relations, 1630 to 1784* (McGill-Queen's University Press, Montreal, 1973), and in Gordon Stewart and G.A. Rawlyk, *A People Highly Favored of God: The Nova Scotia Yankees and the American Revolution* (Macmillan, Toronto, 1972).

The question of Loyalist settlement in peninsular Nova Scotia is well treated in Neil MacKinnon, *This Unfriendly Soil: The Loyalist Experience in Nova Scotia, 1783-1791* (Kingston and Montreal, 1986), and in a number of articles by the same author: "Nova Scotia Loyalists," *Histoire*

sociale/Social History, 4 (1969), pp. 17-48; "The Changing Attitudes of the
Nova Scotia Loyalists to the United States, 1783-1791," *Acadiensis*, 2 (Spring
1973), pp. 43-54; "The Loyalists: 'A Different People'," in Douglas F.
Campbell, ed., *Banked Fires: The Ethnics of Nova Scotia* (Scribblers' Press,
Port Credit, Ont., 1978), pp. 69-92; "Bitter Verse: Poetry, Verse, and Song
of the American Loyalists in Nova Scotia," *Dalhousie Review*, 65 (1985-6),
pp. 111-21. See also the fine local study of Shelburne by Marion Robertson:
King's Bounty: A History of Early Shelburne, Nova Scotia (Nova Scotia
Museum, Halifax, 1983). New Brunswick Loyalist settlement has been
studied widely, but two essential works are Esther Clark Wright, *The
Loyalists of New Brunswick* (Brunswick Press, Fredericton, 1955), and W.S.
MacNutt, *New Brunswick: A History, 1784-1867* (Macmillan, Toronto, 1963).
Two fine recent studies approach the New Brunswick Loyalists from
different perspectives, and have a considerable combined force: D.G. Bell,
Early Loyalist Saint John: The Origin of New Brunswick Politics, 1783-1786
(New Ireland Press, Fredericton, 1983); and Ann Gorman Condon, *The
Envy of the American States: The Loyalist Dream for New Brunswick* (New
Ireland Press, Fredericton, 1984).

The Loyalists in the two island colonies have not traditionally received
as much attention as those on the mainland, but in recent years some
important work has been done. An excellent starting point for Cape Breton
is Robert J. Morgan, "The Loyalists in Cape Breton," *Dalhousie Review*,
55 (1975-6), pp. 5-22, reprinted in Don Macgillivray and Brian Tennyson,
eds., *Cape Breton Historical Essays* (College of Cape Breton Press, Sydney,
1980), pp. 18-30. For the Island of St. John, the relevant passages of Andrew
Hill Clark, *Three Centuries and the Island* (UTP, Toronto, 1959) provide
a frame of reference for Loyalist settlement. Essential interpretive
treatments are contained in the articles of J.M. Bumsted, including "The
Origins of the Land Question in Prince Edward Island, 1767-1805,"
Acadiensis, 11 (Autumn 1981), pp. 43-56; and "The Patterson Regime and
the Impact of the American Revolution on the Island of St. John,
1775-1786," *Acadiensis*, 13 (Autumn 1983), pp. 47-67.

The Black Loyalists were also neglected by historians for many years,
but have now begun to receive their due share of attention. See, for
examples, James W. St. G. Walker, *The Black Loyalists: The Search for a
Promised Land in Nova Scotia and Sierra Leone 1783-1870* (Africana
Publishing, New York, 1976); W.A. Spray, *The Blacks in New Brunswick*
(Brunswick Press, Fredericton, 1972); and G.A. Rawlyk, "The
Guysborough Negroes: A Study in Isolation," *Dalhousie Review*, 48 (1968-9),
pp. 24-36. The impact of Loyalists on native people is treated in L.F.S.
Upton, *Micmacs and Colonists: Indian—White Relations in the Maritimes,
1713-1867* (University of British Columbia Press, Vancouver, B.C., 1979),
and in the relevant articles in Bruce G. Trigger, ed., *Handbook of North
American Indians, Volume 15, Northeast* (Smithsonian Institution,
Washington, 1978). Relations between Loyalists and Acadians are still not
as well documented in published works as they should be, but a starting-
point is W.O. Raymond, "The First Governor of New Brunswick and the

Acadians of the River Saint John," *Proceedings and Transactions of the Royal Society of Canada*, 3rd series, 8 (1914), section 2, pp. 415-52; for a valuable reappraisal, see Béatrice C. Craig, "Early French Migrations to Northern Maine, 1785-1850," *Maine Historical Society Quarterly*, 25 (1985-86), pp. 230-47.

Other useful general accounts of Loyalism include Robert S. Allen, ed., *The Loyal Americans: The Military Role of the Loyalist Provincial Corps and Their Settlement in British North America, 1775-1784* (National Museums of Canada, Ottawa, 1983); Wallace Brown and Hereward Senior, *Victorious in Defeat: The Loyalists in Canada* (Methuen, Toronto, 1984); Christopher Moore, *The Loyalists: Revolution, Exile, Settlement* (McClelland and Stewart, Toronto, 1984); and the relevant portions of W.S. MacNutt's standard work, *The Atlantic Provinces: The Emergence of Colonial Society, 1712-1857* (McClelland and Stewart, Toronto, 1965). As in other areas of Canadian history, there is also a strong tradition of Loyalist biography, including such recent works as Phyllis Blakeley and John Grant, eds. *Eleven Exiles: Accounts of Loyalists of the American Revolution* (Dundurn Press, Toronto and Charlottetown, 1982), and Brian C. Cuthbertson, *The Loyalist Governor: Biography of Sir John Wentworth* (Petheric Press, Halifax, 1983). Indispensable are the biographies in the *Dictionary of Canadian Biography*, which offer both factual and interpretive treatments of individuals ranging from colonial governors to more obscure figures whose experience was nevertheless revealing of the historical developments taking place.

THE 1860s:
DECADE OF CONFEDERATION

The Maritime provinces had changed considerably between the end of the 1780s and the opening of the 1860s. Large-scale immigration, especially from the British Isles, had increased population. Economic development had also taken place, partly in the form of cultivation of the land and the export of agricultural produce, but also in the timber trade and in the related areas of wooden shipping and shipbuilding. The mid-nineteenth century, in fact, would come to be seen by later generations as a "Golden Age" of Maritime prosperity.

Whether that romanticized view would be justified, or not, is a separate question. Nevertheless, it is clear enough that the Maritime provinces of this era had felt little need for a close association with the neighbouring province of Canada. The possibility of a union of all British North America had been broached in 1838 by the British government's high commissioner, Lord Durham, and had been met with abrupt condemnation by the Maritime colonies. Some twenty years later, a similar suggestion had been made by the government of the province of Canada, and had also received a cold response. The Canadian proposal evoked opposition in New Brunswick and Nova Scotia, and was ignored by Prince Edward Island. Yet by the time a further ten years had passed, the two mainland provinces — and Cape Breton, which had been reunited with Nova Scotia in 1820 — had entered the Dominion of Canada, and Prince Edward Island's refusal to do so was not as firm as it may have seemed. The decade of the 1860s had obviously brought about a major turning-point, permanently changing the political status of the region. In doing so, the forces at work at this time also altered the direction of the economic and social development of the three provinces.

In terms of population, the Maritime provinces in 1860 had reached the highest point in their history to that time and were still growing. The 1861 census returns showed Nova Scotia with a population of not quite 339,000, New Brunswick just over 252,000, and Prince Edward Island almost 81,000. The regional total of some 672,000 contrasted not only with the numbers at the end of the 1780s, which were probably rather less than one-tenth of the 1861 figure, but also with the 534,000 enumerated in census data of 1851. Furthermore the population continued to grow substantially during the 1860s, reaching some 768,000 in the census of 1871. It is true that these overall figures disguise some underlying trends. Rates of increase were becoming slower, as the large waves of immigration were exhausted. This was evident in Nova Scotia as early as in the 1850s, and appeared in the other two provinces in the 1860s. From 1865 onwards, substantial out-migration from the region was also having its effect. Nevertheless, the Maritime region in the 1860s could still realistically be seen as having a large and growing population.[1]

It was also a diverse population. At the end of the 1780s, there had already been native people, Acadians, early British groups, Foreign Protestants, New Englanders, and Loyalists: the Loyalists being themselves diverse, including such important contingents as Black and Highland Loyalists. The ensuing years, to the mid-nineteenth century, had seen the complexity increase. Immigration of Irish and highland Scots had grown largely, and had brought about the establishment of distinct cultural communities, such as the highland Scottish areas of eastern Nova Scotia, Cape Breton, and Prince Edward Island, or the Irish community in the Miramichi area of New Brunswick. Lowland Scots, Scotch-Irish, and English were less easily distinguishable, but had entered the region in large numbers. Smaller in numbers, but adding to the multicultural character of the region, were Welsh immigrants — as at Cardigan, just north of Fredericton — and the refugees from the War of 1812 who swelled the Black communities in both New Brunswick and Nova Scotia.[2]

This ethnic variety implied diversity in other important areas of life. Major languages spoken in the region included Algonkian (both Micmac, and Maliseet-Passamaquoddy), Acadian French, various forms of English, and both Scottish and Irish Gaelic. The main religious denominations were Catholic, Presbyterian, Church of England, Baptist, and Methodist, and even these were subdivided by theology, ethnicity, or both. There was also variety in geographical and social backgrounds. Most of the people of the

View of Saint John, 1866

region still lived, by the 1860s, in rural areas. These areas differed greatly from one another in terms of the local economies that were made possible by geographical character: from the rich farmlands of the Fundy shore and of river valleys, to the rocky fishing coasts of the Atlantic Ocean and the Gulf of St. Lawrence. There were also major urban areas. The provincial capitals of Halifax (population 25,026 in 1861), Fredericton (5,652), and Charlottetown (6,706), along with the port city of Saint John (27,317), exercised profound social and economic influences over large hinterlands.[3] So to a lesser extent did other centres such as Sydney, Yarmouth, Woodstock, St. Stephen, and Summerside. All had their merchant elites, wielding both economic and political power on a local or provincial scale.

The powerful position enjoyed by merchants at this time was an indication of the importance to the region of export trades. Pre-eminent, especially in New Brunswick, was the timber trade. The related building and export of wooden ships was also important, though perhaps exaggerated in the nostalgic mythology of later eras. Fish exports were important especially to Nova Scotia, while agricultural products from farms there and in Prince Edward Island were traded both within the region and to the Caribbean. Coal was exported to New England from the mines of Cape Breton and mainland Nova Scotia. By the 1860s Maritime merchants were also actively involved in North Atlantic carrying trades. The Maritime merchant fleet was world class in both size and efficiency, and many Maritime vessels plied between the United States, Britain, and Europe, without necessarily touching shore at their home ports in the region.[4]

With trade much more important to the economy than manufacturing industry, at least for the time being, regional society was structured accordingly. The urban working class was not yet concentrated in the large manufacturing units that would become common later in the century. Instead, manufacturing was typically carried on in relatively small workplaces and was closely related to trade, as in such examples as ropeworks or shipyards. In local economies, small enterprises such as tanneries were common in all parts of the region. So was domestic production of home-spun cloth and other necessities. Along with domestic production in rural areas went subsistence farming or fishing, perhaps with surplus for market, and the possibility of wage labour in non-manufacturing pursuits. Cutting lumber was one major source of employment, depending on the available timber resources in particular areas. Going to sea was another, especially for those living in the major ports: "no country," claimed the *Novascotian* newspaper in 1856, "employs comparatively a larger number of native seamen in manning its craft."[5]

In short, as the 1860s opened, Maritime society comprehended a great variety of human experiences. The people of the region varied according to ethnic identity, language, religion, environmental surroundings, social class, and occupation. In some ways, it was a highly localized society, isolated communities having limited contacts one with another. It was a society of profound entrenched inequalities, in which subsistence food production or low-paid wage labour were the only options for many, while some had access to large accumulations of capital and thereby exerted widespread social and economic control. In between were others, such as substantial farmers, retail merchants, or sea captains, who maintained a degree of economic independence without reaching the status of the elite. In its own terms, it was a prosperous society, even though prosperity was unevenly distributed. International trade was expanding rapidly in the mid-century years, and a trading economy such as that of the Maritimes necessarily felt the resulting benefits.

For Maritimers to look back at the mid-nineteenth century as a "Golden Age," therefore, is not an entirely foolish notion. To be sure, it was not a golden age for all. It was not a golden age for, say, the Irish and Scottish lumber gangs who fought with one another on the Miramichi in efforts to safeguard wage levels by staking out territories. It was not a golden age for Black communities trying to survive on the unyielding terrain of Loch Lomond, Guysborough, or Preston. It was not a golden age for the Micmac and Maliseet still in the process of adjusting to conditions on reserves. Yet there was prosperity. Profits were high in shipping trades, so that capital investment in shipping was increasing by as much as 4 per cent each year.[6] The economy was not autonomous, in that it depended heavily on trading links with Great Britain. In that sense, the Maritime ports might be said to have been part of the hinterland of the British economy. There were also important trading links with the New England states, and with the Caribbean. As far as the rest of British North America was concerned, however, a good case could be made for saying that the Maritime provinces had no need for any strong economic ties to these areas further west.

That argument would not have been accepted by all Maritimers. Even at the beginning of the 1860s there was scope for differing opinions about future economic development. Until recently historians have often assumed that the prosperity of the region in the mid-nineteenth century led ultimately to complacency. Overtaken by the new technologies of steam, steel, and coal, the Maritime economy lapsed into impotence and nostalgia, and leadership was given up to more dynamic areas of North America. Modern historical research, however, has largely exploded these assumptions. First of all, it is simply not true to say that the Maritime economy collapsed with the arrival of new technology. Wooden shipping and shipbuilding continued to yield profits into the late years of the century, even though the size of the fleet was gradually scaled down. The 1880s, moreover, saw significant growth in manufacturing industry in many areas of the region. Thus, the Maritime economy would undergo, by century's end, a process of rapid but not chaotic change.[7]

Furthermore it is equally misleading to suggest that Maritimers, even at the height of mid-century prosperity, were blissfully unaware of the technological changes ahead. Railway transportation had come early to Nova Scotia, with the introduction of steam traction on a coal line at Pictou in 1838. Steam-powered sawmills were already being used in New Brunswick timber operations by that time, and would be built in the province from the 1840s on. Already by 1840, the first New Brunswick-manufactured steamship had been completed at the Phoenix foundry in Saint John; steamships were increasingly making their appearance at ports throughout the region, and made regular passenger crossings in summer between Fundy ports and across the Northumberland Strait. Another indication of change lay in the development of coal-mining as a major part of the regional economy. Although by the early 1860s coal was produced mainly for export, the potential for its use in domestic economic development was already clear.[8]

There was still room for debate over what the effects of the new technologies would be, and what development strategies should prevail. Traditional seaborne trades would obviously be affected, and yet wooden ships were still handsomely profitable both to build and to operate. Increased trade with the northeastern United States might be promoted by building the right railway connections, and this possibility was enhanced in 1854 with the inauguration of a form of free trade between the United States and British North America under the terms of the Reciprocity Treaty. Furthermore, a railway link with the province of Canada might lead to the routing of trade away from the St. Lawrence

The *Maggie Hammond*

ports and through the major Atlantic ports of the Maritimes. This was the calculation of the Nova Scotia government in 1853 when it passed legislation to encourage the building of a railway from Halifax to the New Brunswick border, and thus prepared the way for direct government promotion of the concept of an 'Intercolonial' railway.[9]

By 1860, some progress had been made in the building of railways. The line from Halifax to Truro had been completed two years before, and the connection between Saint John and Shediac was made in 1860 itself. Efforts to extend railway connections out of the region, however, had met with frustration. In 1846, the legislatures of New Brunswick and Nova Scotia had jointly invited the government of Great Britain to build a railway from Halifax to Quebec. Daunted by the estimated cost of $3 million, the British colonial secretary had declined in 1850, and ultimately withdrew even an offer to guarantee a loan for the purpose. Also in 1850 both Nova Scotia and New Brunswick governments sent delegates to Portland, Maine, to attend the official launching of the European and North American Railway, to run eastward from Bangor to Saint John and Halifax. Yet by 1860 no construction had been undertaken on the Maine portion of the line, despite heavy New Brunswick government involvement in financing the connection from Saint John to Moncton and Shediac. A private scheme to build a railway from St. Andrews, New Brunswick, to Quebec had managed to build only some 50 kilometres of track.[10]

At the beginning of the 1860s, the Maritime provinces stood in an awkward position. The region's trading economy was doing well, and there seemed every chance that it could soon perform even more impressively. The Reciprocity Treaty was in force, and if the railway network could be expanded, the commercial potential was very great. Nevertheless, expansion of the railway network was not made any easier by the example of the province of Canada, where railways had certainly stimulated the economy but only at the price of massive public debts. Were railways really the best way of investing in modern technology? Conventional wisdom said that they were, but difficult decisions inevitably lay ahead for the Maritime provinces, and especially for New Brunswick and Nova Scotia.

Early in the decade of the 1860s, another issue arose that affected both the railway question and the more general question of political connections between the provinces of British North America. The United States was approaching its greatest crisis since the American Revolution — the Civil War. Following the organization of the Confederate states in February 1861, the inauguration of Abraham Lincoln as president in March, and the seizure of Fort Sumter at Charleston, South Carolina, in April, the war between the states gathered force. At first there was considerable sympathy in British North America for the Union (northern) states and their anti-slavery stance. Great Britain, however, took a position of neutrality. To the Union side, this was interpreted as a gesture of hostility, for it recognized the Confederates as one side in a legitimate war, rather than as rebels.

In reality, there was much influential moral support in Britain for the southern states. As well as the dislike of many British political conservatives for the republican institutions of the United States, the British textile industry had strong economic ties with the southern states which supplied raw cotton. These issues came to the fore in November 1861, when the British steamship *Trent* was stopped by a U.S. navy vessel off the Bahamas and two southern agents arrested on their way to Europe. To the Union states, this was a legitimate police action. To Great Britain it was a form of piracy, involving the capture of two innocent passengers on a British ship. For a time, it seemed that war would be the result. Moreover, Lincoln's secretary of state, W.H. Seward, was already on public record as speculating about a possible United States invasion of British North America. To meet the expected threat, the British war office immediately dispatched 14,000 additional troops to defend the colonies, some to the St. Lawrence and others to Saint John, with orders to march overland to Rivière-du-Loup.[11]

The *Trent* affair did not lead to war, and the two southern agents were released on Lincoln's orders shortly afterwards. Nevertheless, it had been a dangerous crisis. One of the effects was to highlight again the question of the Intercolonial Railway. When British forces had been shipped hurriedly to North America in the late fall of 1861, the St. Lawrence had been close to freezing. Some of the troopships had been able to reach Rivière-du-Loup, but the later vessels had had no alternative but to make port in the Maritimes and send the troops on an exhausting overland march. Obviously, in this situation, an Intercolonial Railway would have been an important instrument of defence. In the wake of this realization, and in anticipation that tensions between Britain and the United States would continue, the three provinces of Nova Scotia, New Brunswick, and Canada arrived at a new agreement on railway construction.

In part the initiative had come from the British colonial secretary, the Duke of Newcastle. Well aware of the military advantages the Intercolonial Railway would bring, Newcastle encouraged the colonial governments to renew negotiations. In September 1862 they did so, at a conference of governors and ministers held in Quebec City. The result was agreement that the railway should be jointly financed by the three provinces through which its route would pass. Canada would supply some 42 per cent of the necessary funds, while New Brunswick and Nova Scotia put up 29 per cent each. Immediately approved by Newcastle, the scheme only required refinement of its financial provisions, and yet it was on this seemingly routine matter that the agreement broke down.[12]

The agreement had not been unanimously welcomed in any of the provinces, and prompted a government split in New Brunswick. Attorney-general Albert Smith resigned on 10 October, arguing that the proposed railway would only encumber the province with further burdens of debt. Premier Leonard Tilley persisted, however, and late in the year delegates of all three provinces met in London with W.E. Gladstone, the British finance minister. Gladstone was willing to guarantee the necessary loans for the railway, but only on condition that the provinces set aside a special fund to ensure regular repayments. For the delegates from the province of Canada, financially hard-pressed by existing railway debts, this was too much. Abruptly, they left the conference and did not return.[13]

To what extent the Canadian objections to the British conditions were real, and to what extent they represented an excuse for a general cooling towards the scheme on the part of the Canadian government, was a question debated at the time and never entirely resolved. Canadian enthusiasm may simply have waned as the *Trent* crisis receded further into the past. Be that as it may, the railway advocates in the Maritimes were disappointed and disillusioned. So was Newcastle. In the railway proposal, the colonial secretary had seen an essential precondition for a possible union of all the provinces of British North America, which might ultimately relieve Britain of the responsibility for defending these distant colonies. "I have always been of the opinion," Newcastle had written in July 1862, "that the necessary preliminary to a Legislative Union of the Lower Provinces [the Maritimes] is an Intercolonial Railway, and that the completion of *both* these schemes must precede a Union with Canada."[14] The railway, then Maritime union, then the larger union: these had been Newcastle's priorities. Now, they were rearranged. Maritime union became the immediate goal, to be advocated not only by the colonial office but also by the governors of the three provinces. The governors in turn were able to gain enough support from the provincial governments to arrange for a conference to be held in Charlottetown in September 1864.

The extent of the provinces' commitment to serious discussion of Maritime union in 1864 was open to question. A cynic might have argued that there was only lukewarm support for the idea in Nova Scotia and New Brunswick, as resentment against the province of Canada over the Intercolonial Railway failure began to die down. It was true that the legislatures of the two provinces had indicated in the spring of 1864 their approval of the conference but no great enthusiasm had shown in their discussions. For Prince Edward Island, meanwhile, the year 1864 was much more noteworthy for the formation of the Tenant League — a popular movement aimed at resolving the vexed question of land proprietorship — than for the Charlottetown conference. The Island legislature eventually agreed to the sending of delegates to discuss "the expediency of union" — that is, to consider the principle, rather than to make any firm plans — but nobody pretended that the decision reflected any stronger emotion than the provincial government's desire not to be discourteous to the other provinces. One reason for the eventual selection of Charlottetown as the site was in order to ensure that the Island delegation would in fact be inclined to attend.[15]

Yet the proposed conference had attracted attention in certain places outside the region. The interest and approval of the British colonial office was clear. There was also considerable interest in the province of Canada, which was in the grip of a serious political crisis. The province of Canada had come into existence in 1841, through the amalgamation of Lower Canada and Upper Canada. Lower Canada corresponded to the present province of Quebec, or at least to its heavily-populated southern area, and had a French-speaking majority among its population. Upper Canada was similarly the forerunner of the modern Ontario, and had an overwhelmingly English-speaking population. The unification of the two had been carried out in the aftermath of the two rebellions of 1837, which had pitted popular reform movements against entrenched governing elites in both provinces.

The rebellion in Lower Canada, led by Louis-Joseph Papineau, had caused especial alarm to the British government because it had mobilized substantial popular support and was suppressed only after a series of pitched battles in the Montreal area in late 1837. An investigation soon afterwards by Lord Durham, a leading British radical politician, led to a series of recommendations aimed at curbing the power of the elites. Durham also believed that the *Canadiens* must ultimately be assimilated by the English-speaking population of British North America, and the constitution of the new province of Canada reflected this goal. Although Lower Canada's population of 650,000 was much larger than the 450,000 of Upper Canada, the parliament of the new united province would have an equal number of seats from the two. This ensured an English-speaking majority.

Then, during the 1840s and the early 1850s, a change took place. The old Upper Canada, as a result of large-scale immigration, overtook the former Lower Canada in size of population. This led in turn to calls for "rep by pop" — representation by population — implying a larger number of seats for what was now the more populous part of the province and thus an even larger English-speaking majority. Obviously, this did not appeal to *Canadiens* who had had to put up with under-representation since 1841 and argued that the notion of "rep by pop" should not be introduced now, just because it suited the interests of English-speakers. The result, over time, was a major sectional dispute which in the early 1860s led to the quick collapse of four successive provincial governments. Ultimately, in June 1864, a desperate measure was tried in an effort to resolve the impasse. A coalition government was formed, led by former political enemies: the Conservatives John A. Macdonald and George-Etienne Cartier, and the Reformer George Brown. Their programme was to explore a new possible solution by which the old Upper Canada and the old Lower Canada could both have their own assemblies once again, but without the disruptions of total separation. More specifically, they sought a federated union of all the British colonies in North America.

Eight days after the formation of the "Great Coalition," the province of Canada made a formal request to the three Maritime provinces to be allowed to send a government delegation to the Maritime union conference. Although the three provinces agreed to the request, the Canadian initiative raised the embarrassing point that no place or time had yet been selected, nor the delegates named. Without the Canadian intervention, the conference might never have taken place. Now, however, Charlottetown was agreed as the site, 1 September 1864 as the opening date, and each

Colonial Building, Charlottetown

Maritime province selected five delegates. On the appointed day, they met in the chamber of the P.E.I. Legislative Council with the eight-member Canadian delegation. It was true that the circumstances were not ideal, in that the visiting delegates had to compete for hotel accommodation with the large crowd that was in town for the opening of the first circus to visit Charlottetown for 21 years. At least, though, the conference had begun, which was more than had seemed likely three months earlier.[16]

The events that led from the opening of the Charlottetown conference to the inauguration of the federated Dominion of Canada, less than three years later, have been described often enough that only a brief outline is needed here. The conference was dominated by discussion of the Canadian proposal for a wider federation, rather than focusing on Maritime union. The support for Maritime union had always been questionable, and in some ways the wider federation was more attractive. At least in a federal system the provinces would keep their own legislatures rather than merging them entirely, as would have been the likely implication of Maritime union. Other factors, such as the known support of Great Britain for a union of British North America, the possible

James C. Pope   Samuel Leonard Tilley

defence advantages of the scheme in the context of the U.S. Civil War, and the related likelihood of railway development, also contributed. Through reasoned argument as well as through the conviviality of banquets and other social occasions, a strong pro-Confederate spirit developed.

The Charlottetown meetings concluded with the calling of a further conference to be held in Quebec City in October. This time the explicit purpose was to discuss the federation of British North America. The 33 delegates represented not only the province of Canada and the three Maritime provinces but also Newfoundland, the only eastern colony which had not been invited to Charlottetown. In just over two weeks, the conference produced a detailed plan for federation in the form of 72 resolutions. Some had been controversial — such as the proposed composition of the federal House of Commons and Senate — and had been carried only over strong opposition. The Prince Edward Island delegates, arguing from the difficult position of representing the province with the smallest population, were especially unhappy with the allocation of legislative seats. Yet all delegates managed to speak favourably of the federation proposal, and the Quebec resolutions formed the basis of the British North America Act of 1867, which created the new Dominion.

Albert J. Smith

Charles Tupper

Joseph Howe

The Quebec resolutions were refined by a further constitutional conference held in London, starting in December 1866. Yet the most important debates, between October 1864 and the implementation of the British North America Act on 1 July 1867, were not those that took place in London. Rather, the fate of the federation proposals was determined in the debates within the Maritime provinces in 1865 and 1866. There was no doubt that the province of Canada would be in favour of the union, despite disputes over some issues such as the principle of separate schools for Ontario Catholics and Quebec Protestants. This issue was resolved at the London conference, with guarantees for separate schools in both provinces. The status of Newfoundland was still doubtful, even in 1867. Although the Newfoundland delegates at the Quebec conference had favoured participation in the new union, the ultimate decision of the Newfoundland electorate in 1869 was negative. Only after another eighty years would Newfoundland become part of Canada. From the point of view of the pro-Confederates, Newfoundland's geographical position meant that its non-participation was not a crucial blow. The Maritimes, however — or at least the mainland portion of the region — could make or break the scheme. Well into 1866 it had been unclear which it would be.

The question was least controversial in Prince Edward Island, at least in the realm of general public debate. Economically self-sufficient through agriculture and trading connections, the Island apparently had little to gain from new connections with the mainland. Politically it had much to lose — or so the anti-Confederates argued — by giving up its autonomous status to be a small and uninfluential part of a large federation. As put by the leading anti-Confederate Cornelius Howatt in 1866, it was "a question of self or no self."[17]

Strong support for Confederation did exist within the leadership of the Conservative party. In 1864, the provincial premier, John Hamilton Gray, had chaired the Charlottetown conference and had become a convinced pro-Confederate. He retained this stance at the Quebec conference despite reservations about the legislative representation offered to the Island in the Quebec resolutions. Also a supporter was the colonial secretary, William Pope. Just as vehement in his opposition, however, was yet another veteran of both conferences, the attorney-general Edward Palmer. This deep division within Cabinet led to the resignation of both Gray and Palmer by early 1865.[18]

The new premier, James Pope — younger brother of William — had taken an ambiguous position on the Confederation issue, and had not been a delegate to either conference. In the spring of 1865, he clashed publicly with his brother, who was still advocating acceptance of the Quebec resolutions. In 1866, while William was absent on a trade mission to South America, James successfully introduced his "No Terms" resolution in the Island assembly. Prince Edward Island was thereby committed to the view that no possible agreement could be reached that would make Confederation acceptable. Time would show that James Pope's personal views were not accurately reflected by this uncompromising resolution which he had proposed under strong public and political pressure. Nevertheless, for the time being Confederation was a dead issue in Prince Edward Island. In the ensuing provincial election campaign of 1867, it was discussed only insofar as candidates competed with each other in their denunciations of the damage the proposed union would have done to the Island.[19]

As early as in 1865 the voters of New Brunswick had taken a similar view. The pro-Confederate government of Leonard Tilley had met a decisive electoral defeat at the hands of the anti-Confederates who contended — in the words of their leader, Albert Smith — that the Confederation scheme was a product of "the oily brains of the Canadians."[20] The new house of assembly included 28 anti-Confederates, only nine pro-Confederates, and four whose allegiance was doubtful. In New Brunswick, as in Prince Edward Island, the issue was apparently settled.

Yet in reality, matters here were not so simple. For one thing, New Brunswick was essential to the Confederation scheme. To unite the province of Canada only with Nova Scotia, leaving a gap between, was inconceivable. That the British colonial office was committed to the union meant that the lieutenant-governor, Arthur Hamilton Gordon, would continue to work to reverse the new government's direction. Gordon, who personally disliked Smith, had become a strong advocate of Maritime union in 1863, and then of the wider federation. Son of a former British prime minister, Lord Aberdeen, and for a time private secretary to W.E. Gladstone, he was no political neophyte.[21]

In planning an attack on the anti-Confederate government, Gordon soon found that good ammunition was available. In the election campaign of 1865, Smith had placed heavy emphasis on New Brunswick's access to trade with the United States through the Reciprocity Treaty, which Confederation would jeopardize.

Soon after the election, the United States gave formal notice that it would abrogate the treaty in the following year. Furthermore, in early 1866, the possibility arose of military invasion from the United States. The threat came not from the U.S. army as such, but from the Fenians. American-based Irish nationalists, the Fenians had originally hoped to prompt a revolution in Ireland during the 1860s, but had found organizational problems hard to overcome. As an interim measure, the majority among them decided to strike at British North America; by early April of 1866 their forces were gathering on the Maine-New Brunswick border. Heavily armed, and including many veterans of the recently-ended Civil War, their threat had to be taken seriously. In the face of these developments, the possible economic and defensive advantages of Confederation rapidly became more attractive.

It was in April 1866 that Gordon threw down a direct challenge to the premier. Even Smith had been wavering on the Confederation issue, in view of the changed circumstances and the related shift in public opinion, but he was still a long way from taking a pro-Confederate stand. The upper house of the legislature, the legislative council, was staunchly in favor of the union — naturally enough, since its members were British-appointed — and said so in a formal address to the crown on 7 April. Gordon's normal course as lieutenant-governor would have been to consult with the elected government and do nothing without its approval. Instead he chose to accept the legislative council's address. This was a formal action that meant little in itself, but was a direct insult and challenge to Smith and his government colleagues. Smith, perhaps foolishly, chose to resign in protest, and the resulting constitutional crisis led to a further general election in late May 1866. Helped by the fears aroused when the Fenians did briefly cross the border on 21 April — even though only a customs house on the small offshore Indian Island, in Charlotte County, was captured — and by a resulting wave of anti-American and pro-British emotion, the pro-Confederates under Tilley were overwhelmingly returned to power.[22]

Thus, when the votes were fully counted in June 1866, New Brunswick was securely corralled in the Confederationist fold. In Nova Scotia at the same time, the anti-Confederate campaign was just gathering force under the leadership of Joseph Howe. Howe, a former provincial premier and veteran reformer, had taken no visible part in the Confederation debate — though he had contributed anonymous letters to the Halifax *Morning Chronicle* — before his release from a public service position as imperial fishery commissioner in March 1866. In the following month, the pro-Confederate premier, Charles Tupper, used his majority in the provincial assembly to gain approval in principle of the Confederation proposal. Howe and his supporters then started a vigorous campaign to prevent the translation of this assembly vote into the actual loss of Nova Scotia's autonomy. At public meetings throughout the province, and on an extended lobbying visit to Great Britain from July 1866 to May 1867, they put both reasoned and emotional arguments to support their case.[23]

It was a lost cause, even though a popular one. Tupper well knew that the Confederation proposal did not enjoy majority public support in Nova Scotia. Tupper also knew, however, that there was a good chance that Confederation could be a *fait accompli* before he had to call a general election. The provincial assembly did not have to be dissolved until June 1867, with an election to follow some weeks later, and the premier had no intention of facing the electorate on the Confederation proposal. In the absence of an election, as Howe and others angrily declared, the opposition had no way of forcing the issue. Neither was their sojourn in Britain likely to be helpful, in the face of the known British support for union. The assembly's vote of April 1866 was enough to carry the province into the Dominion of Canada and even the presence in some places of black crepe — symbolic of mourning — among the celebration flags on 1 July 1867 did nothing to alter the reality.[24]

But then the anti-Confederates had their chance. September 1867 saw two general election campaigns in Nova Scotia, one federal and one provincial. Provincially, 36 "repeal" members were elected — they were pledged to work for the repeal of the British North America Act, and thus for the dismantling of the Dominion of Canada — and only two pro-Confederates. In the federal election 18 out of 19 successful candidates were anti-Confederates, including Joseph Howe. Charles Tupper, having resigned as premier to run federally, was the lone pro-Confederate member of Parliament from the province, elected in his home county of Cumberland.

For a while events moved quickly. The Nova Scotia assembly formally petitioned for repeal in February 1868, and the petition was taken to London the following month by Howe and others. The hard fact was, however, that the government of Great Britain had no intention of listening. The new colonial secretary, the Duke of Buckingham, explained that the British Parliament had had every right to pass the British North America Act, and that *at the time* the approval of the assemblies of all the affected colonies had been given. Although the Nova Scotia petition was put to a parliamentary vote and gathered a few supporters, the outcome was never in serious doubt. Howe returned to Nova Scotia disillusioned, assisted in negotiating a face-saving "better terms" agreement with the federal government, and in January 1869 joined the federal cabinet. The provincial government persisted in its anti-Confederate stance for another five years, but without practical result.[25]

Thus, untidily and without real enthusiasm, two of the three Maritime provinces were gathered into the Dominion of Canada. Prince Edward Island followed in 1873, its economic stability threatened by railway-building debts incurred in the two preceding years. It would seem that all the evidence exists for a crushing indictment of the way in which the Maritimes entered Confederation. Pressured by the needs of the adjoining province of Canada, dragooned and manipulated by the self-interested government of Great Britain, buffeted by the indirect effects of the U.S. Civil War, these provinces were surely forced into a federation scheme that did not represent their true wishes or interests? Nova Scotia would be the clearest case, with an unscrupulous government refusing to call an election that it could not have won. In New Brunswick the anti-Confederate decision of 1865 was overturned only by byzantine maneuvering by the lieutenant-governor and a freakish wave of emotion arising from the likelihood of military invasion. Prince Edward Island, meanwhile, bravely went its own way, but would soon fall prey to the lure of a doomed attempt to compete with Canada by entering the railway age, and to the blandishments of the Canadian federal government that offered with barbed generosity to come to its aid in 1873.

This interpretation has its elements of truth. It would be difficult to argue that any of the Maritime provinces entered Confederation through an unambiguous expression of popular approval. New Brunswick and Nova Scotia, because they were essential to a scheme that involved the common self-interest of Great Britain and the province of Canada, were subjected to especially strong pressures. Nevertheless, to explain the developments of the 1860s purely in terms of external pressure is to ignore important evidence. Ultimately this interpretation runs the risk of underestimating the seriousness of the crisis faced by the region in this decade.

The reality is that there was deep division within all the provinces as to the direction that future economic and political development should take. That Confederation would mean a loss of political autonomy was clear enough and was reflected in the rhetoric of opposition movements, especially in Nova Scotia and Prince Edward Island. Yet Confederation also implied a specific approach to economic development, based on the construction of the intercolonial railway. For all Maritimers, the choice for or against this approach would have profound consequences. For the capital-owning class which actually wielded political and economic power, the choice was especially difficult.

Part of the difficulty arose from the fact that there was no single Maritime economy. There was, arguably, a dominant economy in the form of the complex of export trades, and related activities such as timbercutting and shipbuilding, that were so prosperous as the 1860s began. Nevertheless, it was clear for all to see that new steam and steel technologies would exert a profound influence in future years. The realization that this was so was partly reflected in railway construction prior to Confederation, and in the beginnings of a different kind of economy in some areas of the region. This new economy included exploitation of the rich coalfields of Nova Scotia and, to a lesser extent, New Brunswick. During the life of the Reciprocity Treaty, coal exports to the United States from Nova Scotia increased dramatically, and by 1865 comprised over 30 per cent of the province's total exports.[26] Development of New Brunswick's Grand Lake coalfield was on a more modest scale, yet exports grew to a significant annual value of almost £34,000 by 1859.[27]

The distinction between the old and the new economies was not necessarily clear-cut. Coal production, for example, was largely an export industry as long as the Reciprocity Treaty was in force, and can be seen partly as an extension of traditional trading patterns as well as being a new economic force in its own right. What the growth of coal production made strikingly clear, however, was that the Maritime region did have choices to make in shaping future economic developments.

The choices can be summarized in three possible strategies. Not among them was the notion of adhering irrationally to outmoded technologies. Whatever else Maritime merchant capitalists may have been, they were no fools, and the encroaching influence of steel and steam technology was evident to all. One possible approach was to integrate new techniques steadily into the existing trading economy without fundamentally altering its structure. New products such as coal would supplement existing export commodities. New techniques would be used to enhance existing trades, as in the case of steam-driven sawmills used for timber production. The merchant marine would be maintained, with wooden ships retained while they were profitable — as they continued to be on some routes up until century's end — but with the possibility of conversion to steam navigation as economic circumstances dictated. Thus the regional economy would change, but would continue to follow the paths which had already proved successful by the 1860s.

A second possible approach was to promote railway as well as steamship development, together with new manufacturing industries, and to do so on the basis of north-south trading links. The railway would connect the Maritime provinces to New England and New York, while coastal shipping would provide an alternative transportation method to the same market areas. In the era of the Reciprocity Treaty this second approach was clearly compatible with the first: expansion of existing north-south links would be accompanied by the continuation of traditional seaborne trades. To be sure, unless reciprocity were extended to manufactured goods — which the United States was unlikely to agree to — manufacturing industry would be restricted in export potential. Nevertheless, fuelled by the railway and by capital generated from international trade, local industries would flourish by serving the domestic market and by exporting whenever possible.

The third approach was quite different, although again emphasizing railway development and the related growth of manufacturing industry. According to this version of the region's most promising future, the key to development lay in the Intercolonial Railway and in a continental orientation. The United States, politically untrustworthy and an economic predator, could not be relied on as a trading partner. Instead, union with the rest of British North America would bring the solid benefits of an assured market for Maritime industries. With the advantage of large deposits of bituminous coal, the Maritime region could hardly fail to be — as Tupper remarked with regard to Nova Scotia in 1867 — "the great emporium for manufactures in British America."[28]

The debates on the Confederation issue were never, of course, conducted purely on economic grounds, and yet the interplay of these approaches to economic development was clear as an underlying force in each province. In an ideal world, there might

Amos Seaman's steampowered sawmill, Minudie, N.S.

have been no conflict among the three strategies. In the real world of limited capital resources and shifting tariff barriers, choices had to be made. In Nova Scotia the economic debate focused squarely on the conflict of the older trading economy with the newer vision of heavy manufacturing industry based on the Intercolonial Railway. It was no accident that in the elections of 1867, anti-Confederate candidates received the largest majorities in coastal communities heavily committed to the trading economy, while potential industrial areas, such as Tupper's stronghold in Amherst, contributed more significantly to the almost 38 per cent of votes cast which went to the Confederate cause in the federal election.[29]

New Brunswick, sharing a land frontier with the United States, was more clearly influenced by the possibility of economic development based on the north-south rail link. Especially for Saint John and the southern New Brunswick counties, the notion of "Western Extension" — the line from Saint John to Portland, Maine — was an attractive alternative to the Intercolonial route, and was so portrayed by Albert Smith and his anti-Confederate supporters. Western extension also had strong support in Maine, especially as marshalled by the Portland-based railway promoter John A. Poor, and the possibility that New Brunswick might become an economic and eventually a political appendage of the United States was enough to cause some alarm among Nova Scotia pro-Confederates. The announcement of the United States' abrogation of the Reciprocity Treaty in 1865 was a crucial blow to those who favoured western extension over the Intercolonial, but until then the debate had been hard fought.[30]

Prince Edward Island, meanwhile, initially stood aloof from such debates. Secure in its trading economy, and politically preoccupied by the more urgent issues of land reform and religious strife over public support of denominational schools, there seemed little reason for the province to become involved in discussing either the economic or political merits of Confederation. Yet the pro-Confederate faction in the Conservative party had been sensitive to economic arguments from the start: the time would inevitably come, declared William Pope in late 1864, when Prince Edward Island would seek to join "her great and flourishing neighbours."[31] The pro-Confederates also predicted that absorption by the United States was the only realistic long-term alternative to Confederation, and the abrogation of the Reciprocity Treaty added force to their argument. Indeed, in 1869 the Island was visited by a U.S. Congressional committee which came to discuss renewed reciprocity, but eventually submitted a report which hinted strongly at the possibility of annexation.[32]

In the meantime, however, a major shift in Island political alignments was in the making. A split in the Liberal party on the issue of denominational schools brought back James Pope to the premiership, after three years out of office. Pope's position on Confederation had always been unclear, despite his "no terms" resolution of 1866, and by now he was reconciled politically with his brother William. William, as editor of the *Islander* newspaper, continued to advocate both Confederation and the development of the Island's economy through the building of a railway. Whether the construction of the railway from Alberton to Georgetown, begun in 1871 under legislation sponsored by the Pope government, was deliberately calculated to bring Prince Edward Island into Confederation, has never been conclusively established. Certainly, leading anti-Confederates made that charge, when railway debts determined in 1873 that the Island must select either confederation or bankruptcy. What is clear is that by the early 1870s Prince Edward Islanders were debating the relative merits of old and new economies and that, by chance or design, the building of the railway led to the incorporation of the island province into the Dominion of Canada.[33]

Economic analysis of the Confederation debates, therefore, provides a perspective of the decade of the 1860s which differs from the impression left by purely political interpretation. The arguments advanced for and against Confederation in the three provinces were many and varied, and included political and financial issues as well as economic. Nevertheless, when the anti-Confederate Thomas Killam of Yarmouth, Nova Scotia, argued that Confederation would harm the fishery by alienating the traditional markets outside Canada, or when John Longworth made the same point in Prince Edward Island with reference to Island agricultural exports, they were cutting to the heart of the entire Confederation question.[34] So was Albert Smith when he argued for western extension, and the Pictou anti-Confederate Martin Isaac Wilkins, when he contended in 1867 that the prosperity of existing trades offered the best chance of stimulating manufacturing industry, rather than the futile pursuit of wealth through unity with Canada.[35] So, conversely, were Charles Tupper or William Pope when they linked railway communications with Confederation as the means of finding new and lasting sources of economic strength for the Maritimes.

The reality was that the Maritime region in the 1860s faced economic choices that were not only difficult but were so complex and so unpredictable in their consequences that they admitted of no clear-cut answers. Only time and experience would eventually determine what those consequences would be. One result of the uncertainty was to produce odd alliances and odd contrasts. That the intensely pro-British Joseph Howe and the pro-American Albert Smith should be common foes of the Confederation proposal was an unusual conjunction. That Charles Tupper's constituency in Cumberland county, Nova Scotia, and Smith's in Westmorland county, New Brunswick, should take opposite positions on the question was an unusual contrast, given their close neighbourhood and similar economic interests.

The uncertainty over the economic implications of Confederation also reinforced the fact that non-economic issues were still essential to the debates that took place. Questions of political autonomy and its loss, of defence, of loyalty to Great Britain: all were important. So too was outright political maneuvering, and the application of external pressures. To argue that the Maritime provinces were trapped into membership of the Dominion of Canada is tenable enough in a political sense. The underlying truth was, however, that the region had reached a crisis point in the 1860s, where economic decisions had to be made without reliable knowledge of the consequences. That being so, unity was unlikely to be achieved in any of the provinces either for entering confederation or staying out. By the end of the crucial decade of the 1860s, New Brunswick and Nova Scotia had reached their decisions, whether by due political process or not. Prince Edward Island was about to reopen the question that had seemed to be closed in 1866. That all three would soon be included in the new Dominion would inevitably have important results for the region and all its peoples. What the results would be — political, economic, social — was not yet clear.

NOTES

1. See Alan A. Brookes, "Out-Migration from the Maritime Provinces, 1860-1900: Some Preliminary Considerations," *Acadiensis*, 5 (Spring 1976), pp. 28-31; and Patricia A. Thornton, "The Problem of Out-Migration from Atlantic Canada, 1871-1921: A New Look," *Acadiensis*, 15 (Autumn 1985), pp. 5-8.
2. Peter Thomas, ed., "The Ballad of the *Albion*," *Acadiensis*, 11 (Autumn 1981), pp. 83-6; Thomas, *Strangers from a Secret Land: The Voyages of the Brig Albion and the Founding of the First Welsh Settlements in Canada* (Toronto, 1986); W.A. Spray, "The Settlement of Black Refugees in New Brunswick, 1815-1836," *Acadiensis*, 6 (Spring 1977), pp. 64-8; Spray, "Reception of the Irish in New Brunswick," in Cyril J. Byrne and Margaret Harry, eds., *Talamh an Eisc: Canadian and Irish Essays* (Halifax, 1986), pp. 228-49. See also J.M. Bumsted, "Ethnicity and Culture in Maritime Canada," in P.A. Buckner, ed., *Teaching Maritime Studies* (Fredericton, 1986), pp. 66-71, and James Morrison, "Mosaic to Kaleidoscope: Ethnic Culture in the Maritimes," *ibid.*, pp. 72-9.
3. *Year-Book and Almanac of British North America for 1867* (Montreal, 1866), p. 19.
4. Graeme Wynn, "The Maritimes: The Geography of Fragmentation and Underdevelopment," in L.D. McCann, ed., *Heartland and Hinterland: A Geography of Canada* (Scarborough, Ont., 1982), pp. 167-8; Eric W. Sager and Lewis R. Fischer, "Atlantic Canada and the Age of Sail Revisited," *Canadian Historical Review*, 63 (1982), pp. 132-3; Del Muise, "The Making of an Industrial Community: Cape Breton Coal Towns, 1867-1900," in Don Macgillivray and Brian Tennyson, eds., *Cape Breton Historical Essays* (Sydney, 1980), pp. 77-8, 85.
5. Quoted in Judith Fingard, *Jack in Port: Sailortowns of Eastern Canada* (Toronto, 1982), p. 26; see also Wynn, "The Maritimes," pp. 167-8.
6. Sager and Fischer, "Atlantic Canada and the Age of Sail Revisited," p. 145.

7. *Ibid.*, pp. 135-8.
8. Graeme Wynn, *Timber Colony: A Historical Geography of Early Nineteenth Century New Brunswick* (Toronto, 1981), pp. 9, 91-2; T.W. Acheson, "The Great Merchant and Economic Development in Saint John, 1820-1850," *Acadiensis*, 8 (Spring 1979), pp. 14-15; J.S. Martell, "Intercolonial Communications, 1840-1867," in G.A. Rawlyk, ed., *Historical Essays on the Atlantic Provinces* (Toronto, 1967), pp. 179-84; Delphin A. Muise, "The Federal Election of 1867 in Nova Scotia: An Economic Interpretation," *Collections of the Nova Scotia Historical Society*, 36 (1968), pp. 328-9.
9. See Rosemarie Langhout, "Developing Nova Scotia: Railways and Public Accounts, 1848-1867," *Acadiensis*, 14 (Spring 1985), pp. 3-28.
10. MacNutt, *Atlantic Provinces*, pp. 242-7.
11. W.L. Morton, *The Critical Years: The Union of British North America, 1857-1873* (Toronto, 1964), pp. 87-102.
12. *Ibid.*, p. 122.
13. *Ibid.*, pp. 123-4; C.M. Wallace, "Sir Albert James Smith," DCB, XI, 828-9.
14. Quoted in Morton, *The Critical Years*, p. 108.
15. Francis W.P. Bolger, ed., *Canada's Smallest Province: A History of Prince Edward Island* ([Charlottetown], 1973), pp. 137-42; P.B. Waite, "The 1860s," in J.M.S. Careless, ed., *Colonists and Canadiens, 1760-1867*, pp. 257-8; Morton, *Critical Years*, pp. 143-4.
16. Bolger, *Canada's Smallest Province*, pp. 141-6.
17. Quoted in David Weale and Harry Baglole, *The Island and Confederation: The End of an Era* (Summerside, 1973), p. 118.
18. Ian Ross Robertson, "Political Realignment in Pre-Confederation Prince Edward Island, 1863-1870," *Acadiensis*, 15 (Autumn 1985), pp. 36-7; Robertson, "William Henry Pope," DCB, X, 596-7; Robertson, "James Colledge Pope," DCB, XI, 700-1; Robertson, "Edward Palmer," DCB, XI, 667; David E. Weale, "John Hamilton Gray," DCB, XI, 370-1.
19. Robertson, "James Colledge Pope," DCB, XI, 700-1; Weale and Baglole, *The Island and Confederation*, pp. 127-8; F.W.P. Bolger, "Prince Edward Island Rejects Confederation, 1864-1867" in Bolger, *Canada's Smallest Province*, pp. 181-4.
20. Quoted in C.M. Wallace, "Sir Albert James Smith," DCB, XI, 829.
21. W.S. MacNutt, *New Brunswick: A History, 1784-1867* (Toronto, 1963), pp. 393, 414-18.
22. *Ibid.*, pp. 427-54; see also P.M. Toner, "'The Green Ghost': Canada's Fenians and the Raids," *Eire/Ireland*, 16, no. 4 (1981), pp. 27-47.
23. J. Murray Beck, *Joseph Howe: The Briton Becomes Canadian, 1848-1873* (Kingston and Montreal, 1983), pp. 182-218.
24. See Morton, *The Critical Years*, pp. 220-1.
25. K.G. Pryke, *Nova Scotia and Confederation, 1864-74* (Toronto, 1979), pp. 80-188.
26. Muise, "Federal Election of 1867," p. 329.
27. MacNutt, *New Brunswick*, pp. 383-4.

28. Quoted in Muise, "Federal Election of 1867," p. 338.
29. *Ibid.*, pp. 341-2.
30. See Wallace, "Sir Albert Smith," DCB, XI, 829-30; MacNutt, *New Brunswick*, pp. 410-13; A.G. Bailey, "Railways and the Confederation Issue in New Brunswick, 1863-1865," in Bailey, *Culture and Nationality* (Toronto, 1972), pp. 76-92; Brian J. Young, "John Alfred Poor," DCB, X, 591-2.
31. Quoted in Bolger, "Prince Edward Island Rejects Confederation," p. 166.
32. Bolger, "The Coy Maiden Resists, 1867-1872," in Bolger, *Canada's Smallest Province*, pp. 191-3.
33. Robertson, "Political Realignment," pp. 52-8; Robertson, "James Colledge Pope," DCB, XI, 701-2.
34. Muise, "Federal Election of 1867," pp. 345-6; Bolger, "Prince Edward Island Rejects Confederation," pp. 174-5.
35. Harold L. Scammell "Martin Isaac Wilkins: Opponent of Confederation in Canada," *Collections of the Nova Scotia Historical Society*, 36 (1968), pp. 312-16; see also R.A. MacLean, "Martin Isaac Wilkins," DCB, XI, 926-7.

FURTHER
READING

There are many general accounts of the process leading to Confederation, two of the most useful being P.B. Waite, *The Life and Times of Confederation, 1864-1867: Politics, Newspapers, and the Union of British North America* (UTP, Toronto, 1962), and W.L. Morton, *The Critical Years: The Union of British North America, 1857-1873* (McClelland and Stewart, Toronto, 1964). There are also a number of studies which bear on the political, social, and economic characteristics of the Maritime provinces as the Confederation era approached. W.S. MacNutt's *The Atlantic Provinces: The Emergence of Colonial Society* (McClelland and Stewart, Toronto, 1965) ends in 1857 but provides essential background. Other works which deal with social and economic themes, and offer a comparative or thematic approach, cutting across provincial boundaries, are S.A. Saunders, *The Economic History of the Maritime Provinces* (2nd edition, ed. T.W. Acheson; Acadiensis Press, Fredericton, 1984); Alan A. Brookes, "Out-Migration from the Maritime Provinces, 1860-1900: Some Preliminary Considerations," *Acadiensis*, 5 (Spring 1976), pp. 26-55; Patricia A. Thornton, "The Problem of Out-Migration from Atlantic Canada, 1871-1921: A New Look," *Acadiensis*, 15 (Autumn 1985), pp. 3-34; Graeme Wynn, "The Maritimes: The Geography of Fragmentation and Neglect," in L.D. McCann, ed., *Heartland and Hinterland: A Geography of Canada* (Prentice-Hall, Scarborough, Ont., 1982), pp. 156-213; Judith Fingard, *Jack in Port: Sailortowns of Eastern Canada* (UTP, Toronto, 1982); and Eric W. Sager and Lewis R. Fischer, "Atlantic Canada and the Age of Sail Revisited," *Canadian Historical Review*, 63 (1982), pp. 125-50. On the early development of the coal industry, see Del Muise, "The Making of an Industrial Community: Cape Breton Coal Towns, 1867-1900," in Don Macgillivray and Brian Tennyson, eds., *Cape Breton Historical Essays* (College of Cape Breton Press, Sydney, 1980), pp. 76-94.

Otherwise, much of the writing on the 1860s must be sought by focusing on one of the three provinces, although many of the books and articles suggest possible comparisons among them. For Nova Scotia, the political history of Confederation has been well served by recent authors, including Kenneth G. Pryke, *Nova Scotia and Confederation, 1864-1871* (UTP, Toronto, 1979), and the second volume of J. Murray Beck's biography of Joseph Howe: *Joseph Howe: The Briton Becomes Canadian, 1848-1873* (McGill-Queen's University Press, Kingston and Montreal, 1983). There has also been important reinterpretation of the economic background to the Confederation issue in the province, as in Delphin A. Muise, "The Federal Election of 1867 in Nova Scotia: An Economic Interpretation," *Collections of the Nova Scotia Historical Society*, 36 (1968), pp. 327-51; Muise, "Parties and Constituencies: Federal Elections in Nova Scotia, 1867-1896," *Historical Papers, 1971*, pp. 183-202; Brian D. Tennyson, "Economic Nationalism and Confederation: A Case Study in Cape Breton," *Acadiensis*, 2 (Autumn 1972), pp. 39-53; and Rosemarie Langhout, "Developing Nova Scotia: Railways and Public Accounts, 1849-1867," *Acadiensis*, 14 (Spring 1985), pp. 3-28.

On Prince Edward Island, the Confederation era has been extensively treated in the works of Francis W.P. Bolger: *Prince Edward Island and Confederation, 1863-1873* (St. Dunstan's University Press, Charlottetown, 1964), and Bolger, ed., *Canada's Smallest Province: A History of P.E.I.* (P.E.I. Centennial Commission, Charlottetown, 1973). A revisionist approach can be found in David Weale and Harry Baglole, *The Island and Confederation: The End of an Era* (Williams and Crue, Summerside, 1973). Most recently, new light has been shed on the Island's consideration of the Confederation issue by the works of Ian Ross Robertson: notably in "Political Realignment in Pre-Confederation Prince Edward Island, 1863-1870," *Acadiensis* 15 (Autumn 1985), pp. 35-58; and in Robertson's biographies of leading figures such as W.H. and J.C. Pope in the *Dictionary of Canadian Biography*, Volumes X and XI.

New Brunswick has long had a tradition of sophisticated historical writing on the Confederation era, and yet a modern synthesis is still awaited. The standard narrative account is in W.S. MacNutt, *New Brunswick: A History, 1784-1867* (Macmillan, Toronto, 1963). Also important are the articles by A.G. Bailey, collected in section 3 of his *Culture and Nationality: Essays by A.G. Bailey* (McClelland and Stewart, Toronto, 1972), and the fine poem, "Confederation Debate," which is included in the same volume. Important elements of the economic background can be found in Graeme Wynn, *Timber Colony: A Historical Geography of Early Nineteenth Century New Brunswick* (UTP, Toronto, 1981), and T.W. Acheson, *Saint John: The Making of a Colonial Urban Community* (UTP, Toronto, 1985). On the Fenian incursions, see P.M. Toner, " 'The Green Ghost'; Canada's Fenians and the Raids," *Eire/Ireland*, 16, no. 4 (1981), pp. 27-47. Valuable biographical contributions are J.K. Chapman, *The Career of Arthur Hamilton Gordon, First Lord Stanmore, 1829-1912* (UTP, Toronto, 1964), and W.M. Baker, *Timothy Warren Anglin, 1822-1896: Irish Catholic Canadian* (UTP, Toronto, 1977). Biographical treatment of Albert Smith can be found in Carl Wallace, "Albert Smith, Confederation, and Reaction in New Brunswick, 1852-1882," *Canadian Historical Review*, 44 (1963), pp. 285-312, in the more popular work by J.E. Belliveau, *The Spendid Life of Albert*

Smith and the Women he Left Behind (Lancelot Press, Windsor, N.S., 1976), and in Wallace's biography in Volume XI of the *Dictionary of Canadian Biography*. On this entire decade, as on the previous ones, the *Dictionary of Canadian Biography* is an essential source.

THE 1880s:
DECADE OF
INDUSTRY

In the whole of Maritime history there is no more ingrained myth than the idea that, following the "Golden Age" of prosperity in the mid-nineteenth century, this region promptly suffered an economic collapse. Recent research has shown that this is a misinterpretation. Worse still, it is a misinterpretation that has often led to misunderstanding of the predicament of the Maritime economy in more recent times. Because the key to a more accurate perspective lies in the developments of the 1880s, the study of that decade has a special importance. The decade of the 1880s for the Maritime provinces was a time of profound change, not only economically, but socially and culturally as well. Until Maritimers come to grips with the complexities of what happened in that decade, real understanding of later events will be hard to achieve.

In its most extreme form the "Golden Age" interpretation of Maritime economic history holds that the region briefly attained a pinnacle of prosperity in the 1860s. This was the age, as described in a famous phrase by F.W. Wallace in 1924, of "wooden ships and iron men."[1] The Maritimes' merchant fleet was the fourth largest in the world, and the disciplined skills of Bluenose skippers took their vessels to all the major trading ports of the several continents. Unfortunately, so the myth continues, technological change was about to bring this glorious era to an abrupt end. The occasion was the serious downturn in world trade which began in 1873. The real reason, though, was that wood and wind had been supplanted by steel and steam. Tenaciously as the Maritime provinces might try to hang on to the age of sail, the world had moved on. Unable or unwilling to adapt, the Maritimes would henceforth endure a chronic burden of economic problems, lightened only by reflecting on the splendid heritage of a romantic bygone age.

All myths have their elements of truth. Nobody would dispute that the Maritime merchant fleet was a powerful force in mid-nineteenth century world trade. Nobody would dispute that shipowning and shipbuilding were crucially important to the local economies of many Maritime ports at that time. On virtually every other point, however, recent research has shown up the flaws in the traditional interpretation. One major criticism has emerged from the work of the important Maritime History Group at Memorial University of Newfoundland. Through its analysis of shipowning patterns in the leading ports of the Maritimes and Newfoundland, the notion of a sudden economic collapse has been disproved. On the contrary, although wooden shipping declined in importance in the late nineteenth century, healthy profits could still be generated up until the 1890s by some owners and builders. Productivity rates of vessels — based on time taken for voyages, time between each voyage, and crew size — were substantially increased in the final decades of the century, and the normal lifetime of vessels was extended. Thus, although there was a decline after 1873, it was a controlled scaling-down, and not an undignified collapse. Far from adhering blindly to old-fashioned methods, Maritime shipowners shrewdly calculated the ways in which wooden shipping could still be made commercially worthwhile, even though the fleet was contracting steadily.[2]

This is an important point, both in itself and in that it helps to demolish an unwarranted assumption that has all too often been made: namely that Maritimers, and especially Maritime entrepreneurs, were too lethargic or too preoccupied with outmoded traditions to be able to adapt to modern technologies. A further criticism of the "Golden Age" interpretation is just as simple and just as important. The decline of wooden shipping and shipbuilding, such as it was, did not mark the end of economic prosperity for the Maritime provinces. Far from being devastated by the contraction of these traditional sectors of the economy, substantial areas of the region enjoyed unprecedented economic growth during the decade of the 1880s.

Already by the time of the Confederation debates of the 1860s, it had been clear that the Maritime provinces were not likely to fail to adapt to new technologies. Economic development based on steam transportation had, in fact, been central to those debates. Among the implications of the eventual decision of the three provinces to join in the Canadian Confederation was a commitment to the Intercolonial Railway as an agent of development. The 1880s saw the apparent success of this strategy.

As was pointed out in 1972 in an important article by the University of New Brunswick historian T.W. Acheson, the key to this phase of Maritime economic history lay in the federal government's "National Policy."[3] In the federal general election of 1878, the Conservative Party of John A. Macdonald was returned to power after being in opposition for almost five years. During that time the Liberal government of Alexander Mackenzie had attempted (though without success) to negotiate a partial free trade agreement with the United States, and had kept Canadian import tariffs low. Macdonald had a quite different approach. Elected in 1878 on a platform of economic nationalism, his government immediately set about the stimulation of Canadian manufacturing industry by means of tariff barriers standing in the way of foreign imports.

Significantly for the Maritime provinces, the new measures were introduced to Parliament on 14 March by Leonard Tilley. Tilley, the pro-Confederate premier of New Brunswick in the mid-1860s, was now federal minister of finance. His budget imposed tariffs of up to 35 percent on manufactured goods imported into Canada, while many raw materials — such as raw cotton, or hemp for ropemaking — were to be admitted free of any duty. The government's hope was that new manufacturing industries would grow up throughout Canada, based on the availability of cheap raw materials and of a protected market for finished goods.[4]

Also associated with the National Policy was the determination of the government to use railways as a means of promoting development and economic unity throughout the Dominion. The most conspicuous example of this policy was the support given to the completion of the Canadian Pacific Railway to the west coast. More significant for the Maritime provinces was the connection of the Intercolonial Railway with routes in central Canada: the Intercolonial reached Lévis, across the river from Quebec City, in 1879. From the start, the Intercolonial operated a system of freight rates which served its own commercial interests as well as favouring industrial development in the Maritimes, in that relatively low rates stimulated high traffic volume, and goods shipped from the Maritimes to central Canada were charged lesser rates than goods travelling in the other direction.[5] With the assistance of tariff protection, stimulation by the railway and its rate structure, and ready access to a major coalfield, conditions were right for the industrialization of the Maritime provinces.

Accordingly, the 1880s saw industrial growth on a large scale. It was most obvious along the route of the railway, in the growth of major factories in towns such as Moncton, Amherst, Truro and, New Glasgow. By 1891 the Intercolonial's eastward link to Sydney was complete, thus joining up the main industrialized belt within the Maritimes, extending from Moncton to industrial Cape Breton. Also profoundly affected in the 1880s were the major port cities of Nova Scotia and New Brunswick: not only Halifax and Saint John, but also Yarmouth and St. Stephen. Some other, smaller, centres were included also. An example is the development of a large cotton mill at Marysville, just north of Fredericton.

By the mid-1880s, in fact, the Maritime region had become a major Canadian centre of the cotton industry, as well as of other important manufactures. To cite Acheson again, the region by 1885 had eight of Canada's 23 cotton mills, three of five sugar refineries, two of seven ropeworks, and one of three glass works.[6] Also in the process of development was the Nova Scotia iron and steel industry, and related manufacture of foundry goods and products such as railway rolling stock. The sheer scale of the expansion was impressive. In the decade of the 1880s, Nova Scotia increased its industrial output by 66 percent, substantially greater than the 51 percent of Quebec and Ontario. To take a more specific case, the value of the industrial output of the city of Saint John increased by as much as 98 percent during the decade. Saint John was Canada's leading producer of nails and brass products, just as New Glasgow was the leading producer of primary steel, and Yarmouth of cotton yarn.[7]

As a demonstration of the immediate effects of the National Policy, the industrialization of the Maritimes was a striking phenomenon. It was also an apparent vindication of the faith of those who had argued in favour of Confederation. The future lay, they had maintained, in developing contacts with central Canada by means of railway development. Now, in the 1880s, Maritime industries were indeed competing successfully for central Canadian markets. Better still, some of the old trades were being maintained. Raw sugar, for example, was being imported in large quantities from the West Indies, thus in turn strengthening the Caribbean market for Maritime food products such as potatoes and fish. The important Lunenburg fishery on the Grand Banks not only benefited from the Caribbean trade but was also stimulated by the introduction of federal fish bounties in 1882: by offering payments to owners of fishing vessels, based on tonnage, the bounties encouraged the building of large vessels.[8]

Amherst Foundry and Machine Works

In general, considering that the Maritime provinces had only some 20 percent of the Canadian population in 1881 — not quite 871,000 in the census of that year, out of 4.3 million — the developments of the decade opened up an enticing vision. Surely this region could now reasonably expect to continue as one of Canada's largest and most prosperous industrial centres. At the same time, the long-established cultural life of the area, expressed for example in its many colleges and universities, would earn it the same cultural reputation as was enjoyed by New England in the United States. Prosperous and cultivated, Maritime society would be a model for the rest of Canada, and the promises of Confederation would have been richly fulfilled.

Nevertheless, even in the 1880s, there were less pleasant realities to be taken into account. One of them was that industrially-based prosperity for some towns and cities did not mean prosperity for the entire region. Non-industrialized areas of New Brunswick and Nova Scotia, and virtually the entire province of Prince Edward Island, were affected only indirectly, in that the employment opportunities in industrial centres tended to draw away population. Population changes in the region in the 1880s were complex, but some general comments can be made.

First of all the decade was dominated by out-migration, which deprived each province of most of its natural population increase. Nova Scotia, the most industrialized of the three provinces, had an overall population rise of only 2.23 percent between the 1881 and 1891 census. The populations of Prince Edward Island and New Brunswick grew by negligible amounts of 0.18 percent and 0.09 percent respectively.[9]

As might be expected, population patterns *within* the region showed that the industrializing areas were in fact growing rapidly. Cumberland County, Nova Scotia, for example, increased its population by 26.17 percent. Westmorland County, New Brunswick, which included the urban centre of Moncton, increased by 9.88 percent. The picture in many of the rural counties was quite different. Sunbury County, New Brunswick, for example, declined in population by no less than 13.37 percent, while Queen's and Albert counties experienced only slightly lower rates of loss. Antigonish County, Nova Scotia, lost 10.78 percent, while seven other Nova Scotia counties also lost population, and Queen's County, Prince Edward Island, experienced a decline of 4.44 percent.[10]

Clearly, there was a major shift from rural to urban areas. In part, this reflected rural economic changes. Some coastal communities had been affected by the contraction of the shipping and shipbuilding trades; the 1880s brought further disruptions as small inshore fishing fleets were affected by market fluctuations and by steamship competition which made it difficult for Maritime schooners to trade their dried codfish directly to such market areas as the West Indies. Also declining was the traditional lumber trade to Great Britain, and at the same time the overexploitation of New Brunswick's forest resource was becoming evident in the virtual disappearance of the pine and the declining productivity of accessible stands of spruce. Changes in agricultural markets were in progress as well. As long ago as the 1860s, the cancellation of the Reciprocity Treaty with the United States had disrupted the trade in foodstuffs to New England. Now, in the 1880s, technological changes were affecting agriculture. In some ways the changes were beneficial. Fast and regular steam transportation made it easier, for example, to export such commodities as potatoes to the Caribbean or Annapolis Valley apples to Great Britain, and have them arrive in good condition. Canning techniques were also important, in stimulating such industries as the production of condensed milk, and the production of canned fish around the coasts of the coasts of the region. Nevertheless, these and other

Steam transportation, Bridgewater, N.S. on the LaHave River, 1888

new technologies also facilitated competition from distant parts of North America and of the world. Refrigerated steamships could now bring meat from New Zealand. Newly-developed wheatlands in western Canada challenged for grain markets. The 1880s, like other late nineteenth-century decades, comprised a turbulent time for rural areas of the Maritimes, and population shifts reflected this reality.[11]

More generally, the question can be posed as to whether the overall drain of population, largely to the "Boston States," would eventually become an actual cause of regional economic weakness. "By the 1880s," one historian has written, "the exodus had taken on the characteristics of mass migration."[12] Rural Maritimers might leave either because of lack of opportunities at home, or because of the positive attractions of prosperous areas elsewhere. To assess the strength of these "push" and "pull" factors in people's motivations is one of the most difficult tasks of the historian of migration. Whether out-migration was actively harmful to the regional economy, or whether it simply reflected already-existing economic problems, it provides clear evidence that the 1880s was a troubled decade for many areas of the Maritime provinces.

Furthermore, in the long-term, even the prosperity of the industrialized areas was not as secure as the heady days of the early 1880s may have made it seem. The new industries had sprung up quickly. Especially in the smaller urban centres, they were often based on limited capital and on short-term borrowing. As such, they were vulnerable to the effects of short-term economic downturns, and business instability — leading sometimes to failure — was a danger from the start. This in turn led banks in the region to be cautious in their support for industrial development. The Bank of Nova Scotia, for example, was affected by business failures in the single year of 1884 to the extent that its total assets declined from $6.7 million to $5.6 million.[13] Subsequently, the bank steadily increased its involvements outside of the Maritimes, and the logical culmination of the process came with the removal of its general office to Toronto in 1900. For all the high rates of growth of the 1880s — and the subsequent growth in iron and steel, and related sectors, in the 1890s — the Maritime region never generated a strong, central financial structure of its own. By the turn of the century, the region would be paying a heavy price for this failure in the form of takeover of Maritime industries by central Canadian financiers.

In the 1880s, the transformation of the Maritime industrial economy into one dominated by branch plants lay still in the future. Nevertheless, even in this decade the seeds of that development were sown, and the beginnings of actual transfers in ownership had been seen in the acquisition by Montreal interests of such concerns as the Springhill and Parrsboro Rail and Coal Company (1882) and the Londonderry Iron Company (1887).[14] The industrial expansion of the 1880s was real, but it was no great golden dawn of economic stability. Vulnerable in themselves to business failures and takeovers, the industrialized areas could offer no solutions to non-industrialized parts of the region that found themselves hard pressed by other economic changes. No solutions, that is, beyond drawing away their young people to work in urban factories. Industrialization wrought great changes during this decade, but provided no easy answers to the problems of future development.

It is in this context that one of the most important paradoxes of the decade can best be understood. The 1880s, more than any other decade, witnessed the success of the development strategy implied by the Maritime provinces' entry into Confederation. Industrial growth along the route of the Intercolonial Railway was plain for all to see. Yet the 1880s also saw bitter disillusionment with the Canadian Confederation emerge strongly in two of the provinces.

Prince Edward Island received little immediate benefit either from the Intercolonial or from the National Policy. The clearest social phenomenon on the Island in the early 1880s was a drastic increase in out-migration. "In our little Province," commented the Summerside *Pioneer* in May 1881, "there is hardly a town, village or settlement but furnishes its quota to this tide of emigration."[15] In part, the problems faced by Prince Edward Island resulted from the same complex changes in the rural economy as were affecting the other provinces. There was another factor, however, which was both a genuine economic concern and a powerful political issue: the question of transportation. The Confederation agreement of 1873 had provided that the federal government would be responsible for maintaining "efficient" and "continuous" transportation between the Island and the mainland. In the context of the National Policy, which implied that traditional Island trades with Great Britain and New England would now lose significance by comparison with trade within Canada, transport across the Northumberland Strait was all the more important as a trade route. Yet conveyance by the little wooden steamship *Northern Light* was quite evidently neither efficient nor continuous.

In the same spring of 1881 when Islanders were becoming aware of the extent of the exodus of out-migrants, they were also reflecting on a severe winter when the *Northern Light* had proved incapable of coping with ice conditions in the strait. Not only had valuable freight been stranded on both sides, but on one occasion the ship had been caught in mid-voyage for three weeks, leaving passengers to struggle across the ice at great personal risk. The two houses of the provincial legislature decided jointly to confront the federal government on the issue. Citing the handicaps endured by Island businesses, and pointing out that Islanders as Canadian taxpayers were paying for railway developments throughout the country that were bringing them no benefits, the legislature's joint address to parliament demanded that the terms of Confederation be fulfilled in the provision of proper transportation across the strait.[16]

This initiative of 1881 set the scene for a battle between provincial and federal governments which would virtually span the decade. In 1883, a select committee of the federal House of Commons recommended improved steamship service, but its suggestions were shelved by the Macdonald government. The government's own proposal was that it would overhaul and refit the *Northern Light*, and provide another elderly wooden vessel as a back-up. Not surprisingly this was regarded as an insult by the Island government of W.W. Sullivan, even though both it and the federal administration were Conservative party governments. The result in 1884 was an Island demand for $5 million in compensation for past non-fulfillment of the terms of Confederation, and in the following year a threat to appeal directly to Queen Victoria and the British privy council. Continuing federal inaction led Sullivan to travel to London in early 1886 to carry out the threat, to the equal embarrassment of Canadian and British governments. From that point on, the dispute cooled. Prime Minister Macdonald made a personal commitment to ensure that the possibility of a Northumberland Strait tunnel was fully investigated — though, predictably enough, the federal government was soon backing away from involvement in any such project — and in 1888 the *Northern Light* was finally replaced by a steel icebreaker, the *Stanley*. The transportation issue was not laid to rest — the tunnel would still be under discussion a century later — but for the time being the political conflict abated.[17]

The Prince Edward Island transportation dispute in the 1880s, while in one sense forming only part of a long series of federal-provincial conflicts on the issue, was symptomatic of deepseated problems faced by the Island within Confederation. Lacking any significant manufacturing sector, and unlikely to develop one in

Northern Light in ice

view of transportation difficulties, Prince Edward Island lost rather than benefited from the National Policy. Both political debates and newspaper commentaries gave abundant evidence that Islanders were acutely aware of this reality. At the height of the political controversy, in 1885, calls for secession were heard on the floor of the provincial House of Assembly. Although Premier Sullivan avoided going to this extreme, the mood of disillusionment was clear.[18]

It was clear also in Nova Scotia. There, in May 1886, the Liberal government did not shy away from the secession issue. On the contrary, the premier of the province, W.S. Fielding, himself introduced resolutions into the provincial assembly calling for repeal of the British North America Act and the creation of a union of the Maritime provinces separate from the rest of the Dominion of Canada. The pretext for this dramatic initiative was a budgetary dispute with Ottawa, in which the province claimed that the terms of Confederation had left it with inadequate revenues. The real backdrop, however, was as much economic as financial. Aware of the difficulties being experienced by rural and coastal areas of the province, because of the decline of shipbuilding and of fish and agricultural exports, the Fielding government argued that in 1867 Nova Scotia had been maneuvered into joining a

Confederation which did not serve the real economic interests of the province. "I regard Confederation as a *wrong* and a substantial *injury* to Nova Scotia," Fielding declared angrily in a letter of January 1886, shortly after the Macdonald government had brusquely rejected the province's appeal for additional federal grants.[19]

Soon after the repeal resolutions of May 1886, Fielding's government went to the electorate of the province in a general election. It was re-elected with an increased majority. Fielding, interpreting the result as a mandate for seeking repeal, embarked on a campaign to interest the other two provinces in a Maritime union. He had little success — "the island Government is *Tory*, the New Brunswick government is *timid*," he observed in a letter of August 1886 — and a further blow came in the federal election of 1887.[20] Fielding discovered that many of his own Liberal supporters saw the repeal resolutions not as a true call for secession but rather as a bargaining chip in resolving the financial dispute. Worse still, the federal Liberal party under Edward Blake had no intention of burdening itself with support for a policy that would dismantle the Dominion of Canada. Amid the confusion, the Liberals managed to win only seven of Nova Scotia's 21 federal seats. Even Fielding thenceforth reconciled himself to pursuing provincial interests within Confederation rather than advocating repeal.[21]

Nevertheless, the 1886-87 repeal movement in Nova Scotia, like the Prince Edward Island transportation conflict, was revealing of the different interests that co-existed within the Maritimes. Fielding's support in his successful provincial election of 1886 had come largely from those areas hardest hit by the decline of traditional economic pursuits. The areas that had depended upon the old export trades, such as along the southern and eastern shores of the province, had elected pro-repeal Liberals, even in former Conservative strongholds. The industrializing areas along the railway and in Cape Breton, on the other hand, went strongly in favour of continuing membership of Confederation.[22] The economic disparities within the region, which had been foreshadowed in the Confederation debates twenty years before, were now real, acute, and strongly enough felt to emerge as major political issues of the 1880s.

In the more prosperous areas, the progress of industrialization was reflected in manifestations quite different from bitter political disputes over possible secession. For the social elites of those parts of the region, increasing wealth was accompanied by an unprecedented cultural and intellectual flowering. Nowhere was this more true than in southern New Brunswick, where the 1880s saw important cultural developments in both English-speaking and Acadian communities.

In the English-speaking context these developments included both literary expressions and a new consciousness of the region's history. The poets Bliss Carman and Charles G.D. Roberts first made their reputations in this decade, through their celebrations of the natural landscapes and seascapes of New Brunswick and Nova Scotia. Cousins and fellow-graduates of the University of New Brunswick, each of the two would spend many years outside Canada before returning in the 1920s to be acclaimed as a pioneer of the country's literature. Their poetry of the 1880s reflected the non-industrialized past rather than the new industrialism of the region, and yet the evocations of the relationship between change and continuity in poems such as Roberts's "Tantramar Revisited" (1883), and Carman's "Low Tide on Grand Pré" (1886) gave powerful voice to the uncertainties generated in a region entering the throes of rapid social and economic change. Carman's nostalgic sense of loss, over the absence of an unnamed companion and the memory of a shared canoe trip by twilight the previous summer, was woven into an evocation of the sunset in the tidal barrens of Grand Pré, where with "a sigh like driven wind or foam: In grief the flood is bursting home." Time itself, for Carman, was "a grievous stream."[23] Roberts, looking down on the great Tantramar marshes from a high vantage-point, recalled his early memories of sunlit dykes and windswept meadows. Wisely, he decided not to venture down to the marshes themselves, in case his vision of an unchanging landscape should dissolve in the face of reality:

> Yet will I stay my steps
> and not go down to the marshland,
> Muse and recall far off, rather remember than see,
> Lest on too close sight I miss the darling illusion,
> Spy at their task even here
> the hands of chance and change.[24]

Another "darling illusion" that could help to offset the grief and uncertainty caused by turbulent change was the myth of Loyalism. As the Loyalist experience had faded further into the past, so the interest of New Brunswickers in that era of the province's history had steadily declined. In the middle decades of the nineteenth century, one historian has commented, "the image of the Loyalists seems to have progressively faded and blurred."[25] In the 1870s, in reaction to centennial celebrations of the American Revolution, interest in the Loyalists revived to some extent, but it was in the 1880s that the Loyalist heritage began to generate a new enthusiasm. The Loyalist centennial observances in Saint John reached their height on Loyalist Day, 18 May 1883. A church service, a full afternoon of eulogistic speeches, a poetry contest, a re-enactment of the Loyalist landing, and an evening parade, made up the events of the day.[26] In part, the centennial was simply an excuse to celebrate. What was new, however, was the elevation of the Loyalists to a high moral pedestal, together with frequent comparison of their migration with that of the Israelites out of Egypt, and the notion that they were in some sense the founders and architects of Canadian nationhood.[27] At the same time, the Loyalist celebrations demonstrated the fervent emotions of loyalty to the British empire that were essential to the patriotism of English-speaking Canadians of the 1880s, whether expressed as actively as in the dispatch of militiamen to suppress the Riel revolt in the northwestern territories in 1885, or more passively in following the extensive newspaper reports of the exploits of Cecil Rhodes in southern Africa. The Loyalists had suffered for the integrity of the empire in their day, and their memory was venerated now to a degree that even the most idealistic among them would have found surprising.

The Loyalist centennial celebrations had lasting results. Although interest temporarily died down after the centennial year, it revived in the later years of the decade. The New Brunswick Loyalist Society, for example, was founded in May 1889, and annual Loyalist Day observances commenced.[28] Where the linkage of this cultural phenomenon with industrialization became explicit was in references to the current prosperity of New Brunswick as the vindication — even the divine rewarding — of the faith of the Loyalists as they sought to transform the wilderness environment of the province in the 1780s. The Loyalist myth also provided reassurance that the high values of the province's founders had not been forgotten in the scramble for material wealth. The fact was that the old New Brunswick *had* been lost. To assert continuity through celebrating a new version of the Loyalist heritage was a way of cushioning that uncomfortable reality, and of pretending that in a moral sense no basic change had occurred.

Also centred in southern New Brunswick, and also involving a newly-reinterpreted version of history, was the Acadian Renaissance. The term "Acadian Renaissance" has a number of meanings, both general and specific, but is most often used to refer to the reassertion of Acadian national consciousness which proceeded from the first Acadian convention, held at Memramcook, New Brunswick, in July 1881. The roots of the movement lay in a series of earlier events and processes. The publication of Henry Wadsworth Longfellow's poem *Evangeline* in 1847 was one important forerunner. Although intended by Longfellow primarily as a romance of separated lovers, and a celebration of the faithfulness of Evangeline to her lost fiancé, the poem offered a powerful image of the Acadians as a virtuous peasant people cruelly persecuted at the time of the deportation, who nevertheless accepted their fate with Christian fortitude. "Thus dwelt together in love these simple Acadian farmers," wrote Longfellow; "dwelt in the love of God and of man."[29]

Longfellow's poem, like the 1883 image of the Loyalists, had only a tenuous relationship to actual historical experience, but it was quickly adopted by clergymen and others as a cultural tool that could help to fashion a new sense of national identity for Acadians. The experience of the deportation had been met with simple Christian virtue, and now this same moral strength could be used in reuniting the scattered Acadian communities and in opening new opportunities for Acadians both individually and collectively.

As time went on, these early hopes were increasingly realized in specific ways. The foundation of the Collège St-Joseph at Memramcook in 1864 made higher education available to Acadians in their own language. Some three years later, in July 1867, appeared the first French-language newspaper in the Maritimes: the *Moniteur Acadien*, published in Shediac. The following decade saw increased participation of Acadians in political life. The first election of an Acadian to a provincial legislature had been in Nova Scotia as early as the 1830s, but until the 1870s real Acadian political influence in all three provinces had remained weak. The appointment of Pierre-Amand Landry — one of the first students of the Collège St-Joseph — to the New Brunswick cabinet in 1878, as minister of public works, was a genuine breakthrough.[30]

In June 1880, Landry led a delegation of some 70 Acadians to a major conference of French-speaking North Americans, held in Quebec City. Out of this large celebration of francophone culture came the proposal to hold a convention specifically for Acadians at the Collège St-Joseph in the following year. Accordingly, on July 20 and 21, 1881, some 5000 Acadians gathered. Only a few hundred actually participated in the debates, and of those there was a disproportionately large number of clergymen. Nevertheless, the discussions ranged widely, including not only religious and cultural affairs but also political and economic questions. Much attention was given, for example, to debating possible ways of stimulating Acadian agriculture and of reversing the tide of out-migration of young Acadians from rural areas.[31]

Symbolically, the convention's most conspicuous decision was the adoption of Assumption Day (August 15th) as the Acadian national holiday. The selection of a religious feast-day indicated again the influence of the clergy, while the decision *not* to select St-Jean Baptiste Day — the national holiday of Quebec — was a declaration of the distinctive identity of the Acadians. Subsequent conventions held at Miscouche, Prince Edward Island, in 1884, and at Church Point, Nova Scotia, in 1890, continued the process of asserting the new Acadian national spirit in symbolic and other ways. The Miscouche convention, for example, adopted the Acadian flag — the tricolour with papal star — while the 1890 meeting coincided with the opening of a new college, the Collège Ste-Anne at Church Point. The decade of the 1880s also saw the inauguration of two influential new Acadian newspapers: *Le Courrier des Provinces Maritimes*, established in Bathurst in 1885, and *L'Evangéline*, which began at Church Point in 1889 and later moved to Moncton.[32]

Considered as a collective reawakening, the Acadian Renaissance of the 1880s is open to some serious questions. In part, like the Loyalist centennial, it was an exercise in historical myth-making. Heavily influenced by the clergy and by the local Acadian elite of Moncton and south-eastern New Brunswick, it did not necessarily address the concerns of Acadians of other social classes and other geographical areas. The fact remained that in business, in education, and even in the hierarchy of the church, Acadians were under-represented in New Brunswick and even more so in the other two provinces. Yet the events of the 1880s did generate a coherent leadership for Acadian aspirations, even if the struggle for full Acadian participation in all areas of regional life would be carried on far into the twentieth century.

Another struggle which was only beginning in the 1880s was the assertion of a new role for women. Here also symbolic advances were made in the Maritimes in this decade, in the first extensions of voting rights to women and in the field of education. The New Brunswick legislature responded in 1886 to a petitioning campaign, from women in urban centres such as St. Stephen, Moncton, and Saint John, by empowering unmarried or widowed women property-owners to vote in municipal elections. Nova Scotia followed suit in 1887, and Prince Edward Island enacted a similar measure for the city of Charlottetown in the next year; Summerside women would have to wait until 1892. In themselves, these concessions did not greatly alter the male monopoly of the political process, limited as they were to local elections and to a small number of women of property. Nevertheless, suffragists could now argue that women were demonstrably capable of the responsible exercise of political rights.[33]

Women were also visibly worthy of higher education. In 1882, Harriet Starr Stewart graduated from Mount Allison College in Sackville, New Brunswick, and became the first woman to attain a Bachelor of Arts degree in Canada. Other institutions in the region, as well as in other parts of the country, soon followed Mount Allison's lead. New developments were also taking place in the professional opportunities open to educated women. Of the 70 graduates of the Mount Allison Ladies' College between 1881 and 1890, for example, seven became teachers, three became medical doctors, five became missionaries, and one a nurse.[34] This example hardly indicates any sudden radical change in the role of women: most of the graduates did not enter on formal employment, and those who did followed careers considered appropriate to the nurturing qualities of women. Nevertheless, the 1880s did see a widening of opportunities for those women whose social background permitted them to attain higher education.

Fredericton, Saint John, St. Stephen, Moncton, Memramcook, Sackville: all of these southern New Brunswick centres were important in the regional cultural life of the 1880s, and all were within the area of the Maritimes most affected by the railway and industrialization. The cultural expressions of the time gave ample evidence of a variety of responses to the new complexities of an industrial society, whether in the form of a search for roots and continuities, or in the form of embracing new opportunities. The implications of industrialization, however, went beyond those reflected in elite cultures. For all those who bought the books of Carman and Roberts, made speeches on Loyalist or Acadian history, or even opened the way for later generations of women in universities and professions, there were others in the same cities and towns whose place in the class structure did not allow them to do these things. There were others yet, in the increasingly marginal rural areas of the region, who had to choose between leaving home altogether or living their lives in a context of narrowing economic scope.

The social contrasts that became evident during the 1880s in industrializing areas were not peculiar to the Maritime region. Whether in Britain, continental Europe, the United States, or Canada, industrialization wrought profound social changes and heightened class tensions. In Canada, however, and in the Maritimes as elsewhere, the experience was distinctive in one important respect. Because industrialization was so greatly stimulated by the National Policy, starting in 1879, it was an exceptionally rapid process in the Canada of the 1880s. The 1889 majority report of the federal Royal Commission on the Relations of Labour and Capital concisely pointed out the paradoxical results:

> By encouraging the growth of industries in our midst we have become practically a self-contained people, able to produce for ourselves all that is necessary to support life in comfort, and even in some degree of luxury. But it also has to be pointed out that in acquiring the industries at one bound we have also become possessed, just as quickly, of the evils which accompany the factory system .... There seems to be no idea of any obligation existing between the employer and his operatives, any more than the mere payment of wages.[35]

The evils the commissioners had in mind were manifold. Housing crises, arising from migration to cities and towns, found only imperfect solutions in the hurried development of new streets and whole neighbourhoods close to the new factories. Growing alarm was expressed in newspapers and pamphlets over the dangers of alcoholism, crime, and prostitution. In the workplace itself, the royal commission noted that the exploitation of child labour had increased. In New Brunswick and Nova Scotia — the commission did not consider Prince Edward Island — there were

Harriet Starr Stewart

no restrictions whatever on the employment of children in factories. In mines, Nova Scotia regulations outlawed the employment of children under ten years, but did allow boys between ten and twelve to do light work as long as their work week did not exceed sixty hours.[36]

The commission also showed a concern with the exploitation of female labour, though from a perspective that limited the scope of its conclusions. The commissioners were concerned largely with the possible moral dangers to women which they considered to be inherent in factory work. Because their questioning of witnesses reflected this concern, the real character of women's work experience was not fully explored, and issues such as low wages emerged only to a limited extent. Only one-twentieth of the commission's New Brunswick witnesses were women, and one-thirtieth in Nova Scotia. This was much less than women's proportion of the actual industrial workforce: 3,648 (19.5 percent) in New Brunswick, and 5,086 (22.6 percent) in Nova Scotia according to the 1891 census. Important though it was that some women were becoming educational pioneers while others were gaining limited voting rights by virtue of owning property, these achievements must be seen in the context of the industrial, domestic, and farm labour which was the experience of most women in the region.[37]

Similarly, expressions of elite culture in a literary and historical sense require to be placed in the context of the overall experience of wage workers whose cultural life was necessarily influenced by their need to respond collectively to the demands of industrial capitalism. The working-class experience of the 1880s was not uniform. Given the variety of industrial workplaces throughout the region, many of which were locally owned, it was inevitable that conditions would vary. Nevertheless, certain general themes can be outlined.

First of all, workers' autonomy survived strongly not only in craft occupations in city workshops, but also in the mines of Nova Scotia. At the coal-mining town of Springhill, for example, miners played an active role in determining the conditions of production, and influenced management through a system of collective bargaining recognized by both sides. In the years from 1882 to 1886, only four work stoppages occurred in the mine. The institutional expression of this approach to class relations was the Provincial Workmen's Association, founded in Springhill as the Provincial Miners' Assocation in 1879, and taking its more general title in the following year. The P.W.A. expanded steadily during

Workers at Marysville Textile Mill

the 1880s, enrolling not only miners but also dock, foundry, and other factory workers. Although not shy of using the strike weapon if necessary, its central principle was the dignity and autonomy of the worker, and the control of the workplace by workers' values without open conflict when possible. The P.W.A. also proved adept at translating its efforts in the workplace into effective political advocacy in Nova Scotia, reflected in a series of reforms of regulations dealing with mine safety, in the enactment of compulsory arbitration legislation by the Fielding government in 1889, and in the appointment of P.W.A. grand secretary Robert Drummond to the provincial legislative council two years later. The Nova Scotia government, pressured from below, thus attempted to fashion a response to industrialization that went beyond short-term political considerations and embraced the values represented by the P.W.A.[38]

Correspondingly at the local level, a whole community could be mobilized in favour of a working-class cause when local control of workplaces was lost. An example was the St. Croix cotton mill in Milltown, New Brunswick, which passed into United States ownership and management when local capital proved insufficient in the early 1880s. During an 1886 strike at Milltown over hours, wages, and working conditions, the strikers' position "elected the sympathy of the entire community," according to the local newspaper.[39] Even so, community pressure in Milltown was not strong enough to prevent the dismissal of one-third of the workforce of the St. Croix mill shortly after the conclusion of the 1886 strike. In the long term, the P.W.A. would face internal disputes and ultimate decline as its characteristic affirmations of workers' dignity came to be seen as inadequate to cope with the influx of large, outside-owned companies to the region in the turn-of-the-century period. The alliance between labour and the state temporarily essayed in Nova Scotia would also wither away. The 1880s, however, comprised in this sense a transitional decade. Industrialization sharpened class tensions, yet working-class and community-based culture and values remained a strong force, if not always a successful one, in determining the character of workplaces and thus of entire communities. The New Brunswick Loyalist Society and the Provincial Workmen's Association were quite different organizations in membership and functions. Each, however, was a powerful representation of culture, and of social class, in the region.

If industrialization brought complexities of experience to many communities large and small, then so too did lack of industrialization in those areas of the region that remained rural and, increasingly, marginal. Out-migration was an obvious expression of the dilemma faced by many rural Maritimers of the 1880s. The dilemma was especially great for Acadians, and provides a wider context to the Acadian Renaissance. At this time, the Acadian birth rate was high. It was high enough, in fact, that the Acadian percentage of the Maritime population grew from 12.5 percent in 1881 to 15.5 percent in 1901.[40] The consequent overpopulation of rural communities, however, led to a level of out-migration that one Acadian newspaper editorial in 1902 described as "another deportation . . . the Acadians being this time their own torturers."[41]

What did the leaders of the Acadian Renaissance have to suggest? In a word, "colonization": the establishment of new agricultural communities as a way of providing for surplus population while also preserving the virtues that were supposedly part of agricultural life. Colonization had been attempted in a number of areas of northern New Brunswick in the 1870s as the opening of the railway had made new lands accessible. New communities such as Rogersville, Acadieville, and Paquetville had been the result. In 1881, a formal society was launched to promote the ideal of colonization, led by Marcel-François Richard, one of the clerical leaders of the Acadian Renaissance.[42] Yet colonization rarely achieved its objectives. Far from preserving a pure agricultural life, the colonized communities often depended economically on work in the woods, or on railway-related employment. Established on marginal land, and with options limited by the control exercised by the major timber companies over large areas of territory in this part of the province, they typically found that agriculture was possible only at the barest subsistence level. Ultimately colonization was unable to cope with the real Acadian problems of an area such as northern New Brunswick: rural poverty, lack of workers' organization in either forest or fisheries, and economic underdevelopment by comparison with the industrialized areas. That the nationalism of the Memramcook convention of 1881 was a real and creative force was beyond doubt. Nevertheless, like the Loyalist centennial and the graduation of Harriet Starr Stewart, it represented an elite culture that was prevented by the constraints both of geography and of social class from reflecting any general experience common to all Maritimers.

For the Maritime provinces, the experiences of the 1880s were complex. Above all, this was the decade of the region's partial industrialization. That fact affected the life of every Maritimer of the time, whether directly or indirectly. That industrial development had now come to be essential to the regional economy meant that the lives of all future Maritimers would continue to be affected by the events of the 1880s. Not only the economy had been transformed, but also the landscape, and the social and cultural character of Maritime communities.

Whether or not these changes were beneficial was a matter of interpretation. Any verdict would depend a great deal on who was asked, and where he or she lived. At best, a strong case could be made for saying that the 1880s represented real progress, that cherished ideal of the Victorian age. This region had emerged, after the inauguration of the National Policy, as one of the leading industrial areas of Canada. In this respect the potential of the Confederation agreement — perceived by only some of the region's leaders twenty years before — had been abundantly realized. Given the healthy developments of the decade, the ready availability of coal, and the continuing expansion of Nova Scotia's steel industry in the 1890s, a bright future seemed to beckon. The Maritime region of Canada might well attain a character similar to that of New England in the United States. Industrially powerful, but also with other important economic sectors such as agriculture, fisheries, and forestry, the Maritime provinces would boast a society and a culture unequalled elsewhere in the Dominion.

Nevertheless, an opposite case could also be argued. Did not massive out-migration, and the bitter disillusionment with Confederation that was evident in Prince Edward Island and non-industrialized parts of Nova Scotia, tell their own story? International market trends were undermining the stability of rural areas, but so too were the disparities between those areas and the industrialized parts of the region. It was all very well to commit the future to factories that allowed the Maritimes to claim the leading producers in Canada of primary steel, or nails, or cotton yarn; but how stable were these new industries in the long term? Given the crop of business failures that had been produced by market cycles even in the 1880s, how far could continuing local control be assured? If local control were lost, as in the case of the Milltown cotton mill, the results might be threatening not only for the working class but ultimately for the entire industrial structure of the region.

By the end of the 1880s there was no conclusive answer to whether the optimistic or the pessimistic view would prove justified. What was unquestionable, though, was that the developments of the decade had permanently changed the Maritime provinces. Whatever the long-term effects of industrialization might be, there was no turning back. Industry and its social implications had entered the fabric of the region. Far from having lapsed into a comatose state after the decline of the "Golden Age," the region had undergone rapid change and bristled with new complexities. The meanings of social class, gender, and ethnic identity, had all been altered in the cultural upheaval of the time. For better or worse, the Maritime provinces — just as the advocates of Confederation had envisaged in the 1860s — had entered the industrial age, and had entered it on the basis of railway development and east-west trade. Would the change be, as the Nova Scotia repealer James A. Fraser declared in 1885, "suicidal to their [the Maritimes'] united interests?"[43] Only time would tell.

NOTES

1. F.W. Wallace, *Wooden Ships and Iron Men* (London, 1924).
2. For a summary of this research, see Sager and Fischer, "Atlantic Canada and the Age of Sail Revisited"; also Rosemary E. Ommer, "The Decline of the Eastern Canadian Shipping Industry, 1880-95," *Journal of Transport History*, 3rd series, 5, No. 1 (1984), pp. 25-44.
3. T.W. Acheson, "The National Policy and the Industrialization of the Maritimes, 1880-1914," *Acadiensis*, 1 (Spring 1972), pp. 3-28.
4. For more detailed discussion, see P.B. Waite, *Canada, 1874-1896: Arduous Destiny* (Toronto, 1971), pp. 101-3.
5. Ernest R. Forbes, "Misguided Symmetry: The Destruction of Regional Transportation Policy for the Maritimes," in David Jay Bercuson, ed., *Canada and the Burden of Unity* (Toronto, 1977), pp. 61-3; Ken Cruikshank, "The People's Railway: The Intercolonial Railway and the Canadian Public Enterprise Experience," *Acadiensis*, 16 (Autumn 1986), pp. 87-91.
6. Acheson, "National Policy and the Industrialization of the Maritimes," p. 14.
7. *Ibid.*, pp. 3-5, 14.
8. S.A. Saunders, *The Economic History of the Maritime Provinces*, ed. T.W. Acheson (Fredericton, 1984), p. 29; B.A. Balcom, *History of the Lunenburg Fishing Industry* (Lunenburg, N.S., 1977), pp. 25-33.
9. Brookes, "Out-Migration from the Maritime Provinces," p. 2.
10. *Ibid.*
11. See Saunders, *Economic History*, pp. 29, 61-3; Alan A. Brookes, "The Golden Age and the Exodus: The Case of Canning, Kings County," *Acadiensis*, 11 (Autumn 1981), pp. 57-82; Margaret Conrad, "Apple Blossom Time in the Annapolis Valley, 1880-1957," *Acadiensis*, 9 (Spring 1980), pp. 14-16; Ruth Fulton Grant, *The Canadian Atlantic Fishery* (Toronto, 1934), pp. 19-24; New Brunswick Provincial Archives, *The Wood Industries of New Brunswick in 1897* (Fredericton, 1969), pp. 1, 17.

12. Brookes, "Out-Migration from the Maritime Provinces," p. 31; see also Thornton, "The Problem of Out-Migration from Atlantic Canada," pp. 3-34.

13. James D. Frost, "The 'Nationalization' of the Bank of Nova Scotia, 1880-1910," *Acadiensis*, 12 (Autumn 1982), pp. 8-10.

14. L.D. McCann, "The Mercantile-Industrial Transition in the Metal Towns of Pictou County, 1857-1931," *Acadiensis*, 10 (Spring 1981), p. 46; Ian McKay, "Industry, Work and Community in the Cumberland Coalfields, 1848-1927" (Ph.D. thesis; Dalhousie University, 1983), pp. 104-5.

15. *Pioneer*, 11 May 1881, quoted in Robert Allan Rankin, *Down at the Shore: A History of Summerside, Prince Edward Island (1752-1945)* (Charlottetown, 1980), p. 126.

16. Mary K. Cullen, "The Transportation Issue, 1873-1973," in Bolger, *Canada's Smallest Province*, pp. 234-6; Parliament of Canada, Sessional Papers, 1886, Vol. 13, No. 76, pp. 34-5.

17. Cullen, "Transportation Issue," pp. 236-44.

18. *Ibid.*, p. 240.

19. Fielding to Edward Blake, 8 January 1886, quoted in Colin D. Howell, "W.S. Fielding and the Repeal Elections of 1886 in Nova Scotia," *Acadiensis*, 8 (Spring 1979), p. 33.

20. Fielding to James A. Fraser, 25 August 1886, *ibid.*, p. 42.

21. *Ibid.*, pp. 41-6.

22. *Ibid.*, pp. 36-40.

23. John Robert Sorfleet, ed., *The Poems of Bliss Carman* (Toronto, 1976), pp. 19-20. See also Sorfleet, "Transcendentalist, Mystic, Evolutionary Idealist: Bliss Carman, 1886-1894," in George Woodcock, ed., *Colony and Confederation: Early Canadian Poets and Their Background* (Vancouver, 1974), pp. 190-4.

24. Desmond Pacey, ed., *The Collected Poems of Sir Charles G.D. Roberts* (Wolfville, 1985), pp. 78-9.

25. Murray Barkley, "The Loyalist Tradition in New Brunswick: The Growth and Evolution of an Historical Myth, 1825-1914," *Acadiensis*, 4 (Spring 1975), p. 21.

26. *Ibid.*, pp. 25-27.

27. *Ibid.*, pp. 25-28.

28. *Ibid.*, p. 38.

29. *The Poetical Works of Longfellow: Oxford Edition* (Oxford, 1912), p. 143; Naomi Griffiths, "Longfellow's *Evangeline*: The Birth and Acceptance of a Legend," *Acadiensis*, 11 (Spring 1982), pp. 28-41.

30. Léon Thériault, "Acadia, 1763-1978: An Historical Synthesis," in Jean Daigle, ed., *The Acadians of the Maritimes: Thematic Studies* (Moncton, 1982), pp. 59, 63-70; G.F.G. Stanley, "The Flowering of the Acadian Renaissance," in David Jay Bercuson and Phillip A. Buckner, eds., *Eastern and Western Perspectives* (Toronto, 1981), pp. 30-1; D.M.M. Stanley, *Au service de deux peuples: Pierre-Amand Landry* (Moncton, 1977), pp. 40-5, 86.

31. Thériault, "Acadia, 1763-1978," p. 71.
32. *Ibid.*, pp. 70-73.
33. *New Brunswick Statutes*, 49 Victoria C.83; *Nova Scotia Statutes*, 50 Victoria C.28; *Prince Edward Island Statutes*, 51 Victoria C.12. See also Catherine L. Cleverdon, *The Woman Suffrage Movement in Canada* (Toronto, 1950), pp. 199-200; Elspeth Tulloch, *We, the Undersigned: A Historical Overview of New Brunswick Women's Political and Legal Status, 1784-1984* (Moncton, 1985), pp. 15, 23; Michael J. Smith, "Female Reformers in Victorian Nova Scotia: Architects of a New Womanhood" (M.A. thesis; Saint Mary's University, 1986), p. 144.
34. John G. Reid, "The Education of Women at Mount Allison, 1854-1914," *Acadiensis*, 12 (Spring 1983), p. 26. The Ladies' College was a diploma-granting school associated with the university-level Mount Allison College.
35. Greg Kealey, ed., *Canada Investigates Industrialism* (Toronto, 1973), p. 4.
36. *Ibid.*, p. 21.
37. Susan Trofimenkoff, "One Hundred and Two Muffled Voices: Canada's Industrial Women in the 1880s," *Atlantis*, 3 (Autumn 1977), pp. 69, 81; Margaret Conrad, *Recording Angels: The Private Chronicles of Women from the Maritime Provinces of Canada, 1750-1950* (Ottawa, 1982), pp. 13-16; Conrad, "Out of the Kitchen and into the Curriculum: Women's Studies in Maritime Canada," in Buckner, *Teaching Maritime Studies*, pp. 110-11.
38. McKay, "Industry, Work and Community in the Cumberland Coalfields," pp. 695-745. See also McKay, "'By Wisdom, Wile, or War': The Provincial Workmen's Assocation and the Struggle for Working-Class Independence in Nova Scotia, 1879-97," *Labour/Le Travail*, 18 (1986), esp. pp. 47-8; and McKay, "The Realm of Uncertainty: The Experience of Work in the Cumberland Coal Mines, 1873-1927," *Acadiensis*, 16 (Autumn 1986), pp. 3-57.
39. *Calais Advertiser*, 3 February 1886, quoted in Peter DeLottinville, "Trouble in the Hives of Industry: The Cotton Industry Comes to Milltown, New Brunswick, 1874-1892," *Historical Papers: Montreal, 1980*, p. 110.
40. Muriel K. Roy, "Settlement and Population Growth in Acadia," in Daigle, *The Acadians of the Maritimes*, p. 170.
41. *L'Impartial*, 10 July 1902, quoted in translation in Jean Daigle, "The Acadians: A People in Search of a Country," in Raymond Breton and Pierre Savard, eds., *The Quebec and Acadian Diaspora in North America* (Toronto, 1982), p. 5.
42. Raymond Mailhot, "Quelques éléments d'histoire économique de la prise de conscience acadienne, 1850-1891," *La Société Historique Acadienne: les cahiers*, 7 (1976), pp. 64,69. See also Michel Roy, *L'Acadie des origines à nos jours: essai de synthèse historique* (Montreal, 1981), pp. 200-05.
43. Quoted in Ernest R. Forbes, *Aspects of Maritime Regionalism, 1867-1927* (Ottawa, 1983), p. 3.

FURTHER READING

Because the importance of the 1880s as a decade in Maritime provinces history has only recently been recognized by historians, much of the relevant writing is in the pages of scholarly journals, rather than in book form. An important general synthesis of the Canadian history of the period can be found in P.B. Waite, *Canada, 1874-1896: Arduous Destiny* (McClelland and Stewart, Toronto, 1971).

Much of the recent writing on the Maritimes in the 1880s has focused on economic issues. The work of Memorial University's Maritime History Group on shipping and shipbuilding has been published in several collections of papers. Synthesis of the group's findings, and bibliography, can be found in Eric W. Sager and Lewis R. Fischer, "Atlantic Canada and the Age of Sail Revisited," *Canadian Historical Review*, 63 (1982), pp. 125-50; in Sager and Fischer, *Shipping and Shipbuilding in Atlantic Canada, 1820-1914* (Canadian Historical Association, Ottawa, 1986); and in Rosemary E. Ommer, "The Decline of the Eastern Canadian Shipping Industry, 1880-95," in *Journal of Transport History*, 3rd series, 5, No. 1 (1984), pp. 25-44. On the new industries in the region, an article of central importance is T.W. Acheson, "The National Policy and the Industrialization of the Maritimes, 1880-1910," *Acadiensis*, 1 (Spring 1972), pp. 3-28; this article was the first to explore fully the implications of the National Policy for Maritime industry. Further insights can be found in several of the essays in David Jay Bercuson, ed., *Canada and the Burden of Unity* (Macmillan, Toronto, 1977); in James D. Frost, "The 'Nationalization' of the Bank of Nova Scotia, 1880-1910," *Acadiensis*, 12 (Autumn 1982), pp. 3-38, and Douglas O. Baldwin, "The Growth and Decline of the Charlottetown Banks, 1854-1906," *Acadiensis*, 15 (Spring 1986), pp. 28-52; in L.D. McCann, "The Mercantile-Industrial Transition in the Metal Towns of Pictou County, 1857-1931," *Acadiensis*, 10 (Spring 1981), pp. 29-64; in Kris Inwood and John Chamard, "Regional Industrial Growth During the 1890s: The Case of the Missing Artisans," *Acadiensis*, 16 (Autumn 1986), pp. 101-17; and in older but still useful works by S.A. Saunders, *The*

Economic History of the Maritime Provinces (2nd edition, ed. T.W. Acheson; Acadiensis Press, Fredericton, 1984), and Ruth Fulton Grant, *The Canadian Atlantic Fishery* (Ryerson, Toronto, 1934).

Population movements had obvious significance in the Maritimes of the 1880s, and an essential starting-point on this question is Alan A. Brookes, "Out-Migration from the Maritime Provinces, 1860-1900: Some Preliminary Considerations," *Acadiensis*, 5 (Spring 1976), pp. 26-55. See also the same author's "The Golden Age and the Exodus: The Case of Canning, Kings County," *Acadiensis*, 11 (Autumn 1981), pp. 57-82. On Acadian population trends, see Muriel K. Roy, "Settlement and Population Growth," in Jean Daigle, ed., *The Acadians of the Maritimes: Thematic Studies* (Centre d'études acadiennes, Moncton, 1982), pp. 125-96. An important recent reappraisal of out-migration patterns is Patricia A. Thornton, "The Problem of Out-Migration from Atlantic Canada, 1871-1921: A New Look," *Acadiensis*, 15 (Autumn 1985), pp. 3-34.

On the politics of the region, and especially the disputes between provincial and federal governments, see Colin D. Howell, "W.S. Fielding and the Repeal Elections of 1886 and 1887 in Nova Scotia," *Acadiensis*, 8 (Spring 1979), pp. 28-46; and Mary K. Cullen, "The Transportation Issue, 1873-1973," in F.W.P. Bolger, ed., *Canada's Smallest Province: A History of Prince Edward Island* (P.E.I. Centennial Commission, Charlottetown, 1973), pp. 232-63. Cultural developments in English-speaking New Brunswick are discussed in A.G. Bailey, "Creative Movements in the Culture of the Maritime Provinces," in Bailey, *Culture and Nationality* (McClelland and Stewart, Toronto, 1972), pp. 44-57; and Murray Barkley, "The Loyalist Tradition in New Brunswick: The Growth and Evolution of an Historical Myth," *Acadiensis*, 4 (Spring 1975), pp. 3-45.

The Acadian Renaissance has been extensively considered by historians in both English and French languages. As well as the essays in Daigle, *The Acadians of the Maritimes*, relevant books in French include Jean-Paul Hautecoeur, *L'Acadie du discours* (Les presses de l'université Laval, Quebec, 1975), Michel Roy, *L'Acadie des origines à nos jours: essai de synthèse historique* (Editions Québec/Amérique, Montreal, 1981), and D.M.M. Stanley, *Au service de deux peuples: Pierre-Amand Landry* (Editions d'Acadie, Moncton, 1977). Also relevant is Raymond Mailhot, "Quelques éléments d'histoire économique de la prise de conscience acadienne, 1850-1891," *La Société Historique Acadienne: les cahiers*, 7 (1976), pp. 49-74. In the English language, see Naomi Griffiths, "Longfellow's *Evangeline*: The Birth and Acceptance of a Legend," *Acadiensis*, 11 (Spring 1982), pp. 28-41; G.F.G. Stanley, "The Flowering of the Acadian Renaissance," in David Jay Bercuson and Phillip A. Buckner, eds. *Eastern and Western Perspectives* (UTP, Toronto, 1981), pp. 19-46; Martin S. Spigelman, "The Acadian Renaissance and the Development of Acadian-Canadian Relations, 1864-1912: 'des frères trop longtemps séparés'" (Ph.D. thesis; Dalhousie University, 1975); and Spigelman, "Survival — New Views on Francophone Minorities in Canada," *Acadiensis*, 7 (Spring 1978), pp. 141-50.

Aspects of the history of women in the Maritimes of the 1880s are considered in Margaret Conrad, *Recording Angels: The Private Chronicles of Women from the Maritime Provinces of Canada, 1750-1950* (Canadian Research Institute for the Advancement of Women, Ottawa, 1982); Linda Kealey, ed., *A Not Unreasonable Claim: Women and Reform in Canada, 1880s-1920s* (Women's Educational Press, Toronto, 1979); John G. Reid, "The Education of Women at Mount Allison, 1854-1914," *Acadiensis*, 12 (Spring 1983), pp. 3-33; Susan Trofimenkoff, "One Hundred and Two Muffled Voices: Canada's Industrial Women in the 1880s," *Atlantis*, 3 (Autumn 1977), pp. 66-82; and Elspeth Tulloch, *We, the Undersigned: A Historical Overview of New Brunswick Women's Political and Legal Status, 1784-1984* (New Brunswick Advisory Council on the Status of Women, Moncton, 1985). See also the evidence presented to the Royal Commission on the Relations of Labour and Capital, as edited in Greg Kealey, ed., *Canada Investigates Industrialism* (UTP, Toronto, 1973).

A stimulating interpretation of the working-class experience of this time can be found in Bryan D. Palmer, *Working-Class Experience: The Rise and Reconstitution of Canadian Labour, 1800-1980* (Butterworth, Toronto, 1983). More specific treatments include Peter De Lottinville, "Trouble in the Hives of Industry: The Cotton Industry Comes to Milltown, New Brunswick, 1879-1892," *Historical Papers: Montreal 1980*, pp. 100-15; Donald MacLeod, "Colliers, Colliery Safety and Workplace Control: The Nova Scotia Experience, 1873 to 1910," *Historical Papers: Vancouver 1983*, pp. 226-53, and a number of works by Ian McKay: "Industry, Work and Community in the Cumberland Coalfields, 1848-1927" (Ph.D. thesis; Dalhousie University, 1983); "Capital and Labour in the Halifax Baking and Confectionery Industry During the Last Half of the Nineteenth Century," *Labour/Le Travailleur*, 3 (1978), pp. 63-108; "The Provincial Workmen's Association: A Brief Survey of Several Problems of Interpretation," in W.J.C. Cherwinski and Gregory S. Kealey, eds., *Lectures in Canadian Labour and Working-Class History* (Committee on Canadian Labour History, St. John's, Nfld., 1985), pp. 127-34; "'By Wisdom, Wile or War': The Provincial Workmen's Association and the Struggle for Working-Class Independence in Nova Scotia, 1879-97," *Labour/Le Travail*, 18 (1986), pp. 13-62; and "The Realm of Uncertainty: The Experience of Work in the Cumberland Coal Mines, 1873-1927," *Acadiensis*, 16 (Autumn 1986), pp. 3-57.

THE 1920s:
DECADE OF STRUGGLE

During the 1920s, the Maritime provinces faced economic disaster. It was in this decade that it became clear that the industrialization of the late nineteenth century had not provided any guarantee of future economic stability. It was in this decade that the foundations were laid for the Maritimes' status as a "have-not" region of Canada. For much of the rest of the country the Great Depression was a phenomenon only of the 1930s. In the Maritimes it began in the summer of 1920 and lasted for a full generation. It was not accepted passively. In settings as diverse as in the mines of Cape Breton, in the small-town universities of the region, in newspaper offices, and in the lobbies of Parliament, the effects of economic decline were resisted with skill and tenacity, though not with success.

There is a myth that portrays Maritimers as docile, quiescent, slow to generate any kind of collective emotion. The events of the 1920s amply demonstrate the falsity of that image. Lacking wealth by comparison with other regions of Canada, losing population whenever there were jobs to be found in more prosperous areas, the Maritimes would henceforth find more difficulty than before in asserting national leadership in political, social, or cultural fields. "As for the Maritime provinces" one of Canada's most prominent historians felt able to remark in 1963 on CBC radio, "nothing, of course, ever happens down there."[1]

Much did happen in the Maritimes in the 1920s, and much has happened since. However, all that has happened since has been influenced by the fact that the economic forces besetting the region in the 1920s were ultimately too strong for those who resisted them.

As the 1920s began the Maritime provinces — like the rest of Canada — were still recovering from the traumas of the First

World War. The adjustment to peacetime conditions, in fact, had worldwide implications, economic as well as social and political. The war had been enormously expensive and yet had stimulated industrial development in all the countries involved. Demand for iron and steel products, as well as for other commodities that had war uses, had been high. As a result the industrialized world emerged from the conflict with more industrial capacity than would be needed in peacetime. This was true in Canada as elsewhere. After a short period of post-war boom, fuelled by the renewed production of peacetime goods, the reality of surplus capacity had to be faced by early 1920.

Furthermore, world trade patterns had been disrupted by the war. Traditional European markets for Newfoundland fish, for example, had been effectively cut off during the war years and were not fully recovered afterwards. One result was that Newfoundland fish exports began increasingly to compete in traditional Nova Scotia markets, such as in the Caribbean. The issue was complicated by the uncertainties of the Caribbean economy, which depended heavily on exports of cane sugar. These exports had been in high demand during the war years, when European beet sugar production had been sharply reduced. Now, beet sugar returned to the world market, and prices declined: as they did, so too did Caribbean purchasing power for Maritime products. Another trade shift, though not so directly connected with the war, was in international markets for timber. Here, the old-established Maritime lumber producers met increasing competition from the newly-opened forest resources of British Columbia. Decreased demand for Maritime sawn lumber was partly offset by developments in pulp and paper, but the overall result was decline.[2]

In grappling with worldwide industrial and trading problems after the First World War, the Maritime provinces were not alone. All major economies of the world were affected. In the Maritimes, however, there were certain factors that made this region's experience unique in Canada. First of all, major changes in industrial organization had taken place since the 1880s. "By 1914," the historian T.W. Acheson has written, "the Maritimes had become a branch-plant economy."[3] The failure to develop an adequate financial structure within the region during the 1880s had led to major takeovers by Montreal and Toronto financiers. In 1881, there had been 274 branch businesses in the Maritimes; the number had grown to 416 by 1901, and to 950 by 1921.[4] Not all of these branches resulted from takeovers. Some represented the construction of new plants by national firms, while others were essentially distribution networks for products manufactured in central Canada. Yet the dramatic increase in the number of branch businesses between 1901 and 1921 did include takeovers in important manufacturing industries, an example being the 1909 amalgamation of the Rhodes, Curry Company of Amherst — one of Canada's leading producers of railway cars — with two Montreal companies to form the Montreal-controlled Canadian Car and Foundry Company.

In stable economic times, outside control might make little obvious difference to the economy. In bad times, such as the early 1920s, branch plants became prime candidates for cutbacks or closure, as companies attempted to cope with excess capacity and reduced demand. Matters were further complicated by the particular difficulties of the Nova Scotia steel industry, which played a key role in the wider regional economy as a consumer of coal and as a supplier of manufacturers of secondary steel products. Chemical and metallurgical problems in the coal and iron ore resources of the region led to increased production costs, which offset the advantage of having these resources close at hand. Also the industry had depended heavily before the First World War on railway expansion, with its demand for products such as rails and axles. Now railway expansion had levelled off, and the age of steam and steel was itself being overtaken by technological changes. These factors made Maritime industries all the more vulnerable to takeovers and to possible eventual retrenchment in favour of plants more centrally located in Canada.[5]

Yet even all of this might not have led to an economic debacle had it not been for another factor entirely: the political decline of the Maritimes as a region within Canada, and the economic consequences of that decline. When Nova Scotia and New Brunswick had entered Confederation in 1867, they had been two of four provinces, and had contained (to use 1871 census figures) 18.7 percent of the Canadian population. By 1891 the Maritime provinces were three out of seven, with 18.2 percent of the overall population. By 1921 they were three of nine, with only 11.4 percent of the national population.[6] This relative decline was faithfully reflected in the number of parliamentary seats allocated to the Maritimes, which were reduced after each census, despite equally regular protests by the provincial governments of the region.[7] As a result, it became increasingly difficult for Maritime political leaders to sustain the region's interests effectively at the federal level. An early indicator of what was to come was a change in 1907 in the National Policy tariff on imports of coal. Already reduced in 1897 from 60 cents per ton to 53 cents per ton, the tariff was now eliminated in cases where coal was used "for the smelting of metals."[8] The tariff had helped Maritime coal to find a ready market in central Canada, and had also encouraged manufacturing firms to locate close to the coalfield. Now, however, it would be easy for iron and steel firms in central Canada to import from the United States, rather than buy from Nova Scotia and New Brunswick.

An even more serious setback for Maritime industry occurred between 1912 and 1923. The freight rate structure of the Intercolonial Railway had always been favourable to shipments of Maritime-produced goods travelling west. Regarded in the Maritimes as a right, and in fact as the only way in which the National Policy could be made to work fairly for the eastern as well as the central areas of Canada, these freight rates nevertheless came under criticism in the early part of the twentieth century. Central Canadian complaints about discrimination in favour of the Maritimes brought about the abolition of the east-west differential in 1912. Western complaints about the general low level of the Intercolonial's freight rates — despite which, the company managed to make a profit more often than not — led to attempts in 1917 to have rates raised to western levels. Ultimately, in a process spanning the years from 1917 to 1923, the Intercolonial was amalgamated with four other railways in different parts of Canada to form the Canadian National Railways. In the same space of time, freight rates in the Maritimes rose between 140 and 216 percent, depending on commodity. The issue had been complicated by disputes within the region, notably between the ports of Halifax and Saint John, as to whether the Intercolonial had favoured some local interests over others. Nevertheless, the result was that the competitive position of all Maritime producers trying to sell in central Canadian markets was effectively undercut.[9]

In the years immediately following the First World War, the Maritime economy suffered a series of heavy blows. In part the problems were worldwide. In the Maritimes, however, the effects of these wider trends were transformed into a major crisis by complicating factors that originated within Canada: outside control of the regional economy, and the inability of outnumbered political representatives to put up an effective defence of regional interests in such crucial areas as tariffs and freight rates. The results were disastrous. In the years between 1920 and 1926, some 42 percent

Robb Engineering Co. Ltd., Amherst, N.S.

of the manufacturing jobs in the region simply disappeared.[10]
Meanwhile, as deindustrialization proceeded, non-manufacturing
sectors such as fisheries, lumber, and agriculture had to deal with
world trade disruption and severe competition in uncertain
markets. There were exceptions. In Nova Scotia, for example, the
decline in exports of salt cod was offset for a time by increased
output of fresh and frozen fish for the New England market. In
New Brunswick, and especially in Prince Edward Island, exports
of seed potatoes prospered as successful efforts were made to
produce disease-free stock at a time when other North American
growing areas were encountering potato blights. Also in Prince
Edward Island, the 1920s saw fox-farming reach its height, as the
market value of silver-fox pelts steadily increased. Yet even in
Prince Edward Island population declined in the 1920s, and rural
population declined more rapidly than urban. There, as in the
other two provinces, many decided to leave — perhaps as much
as one-fifth of the entire population of the region. Those who
remained had to find ways of dealing with the new, harsh
economic climate.[11]

The first group to be directly threatened was the industrial working class. During the early years of the 1920s, industrial Cape Breton became a battlefield as workers resisted wage cuts and layoffs. There were good reasons why this part of the Maritimes would see the most dramatic labour-capital struggle of the decade. The reasons were partly economic, in that the steel and coal production of Cape Breton depended to a large extent on central Canadian markets, and so these industries were acutely sensitive to any alterations in the National Policy as it related to tariffs and freight rates. The 1907 abolition of the import tariff on foreign coal used for metal-smelting was an obvious blow to both coal and steel in Cape Breton. The later increase in freight rates compounded the effect.

The reasons also related to outside ownership of the major industrial plants of Cape Breton. As early as 1893, the Dominion Coal Company had brought control of much of the Sydney coalfield into the hands of investors not only from Nova Scotia but also from New England and Montreal. In 1903 control of the company was sold to a Montreal financier, James Ross. At the same time the related Dominion Iron and Steel Company, with its steel plant in Sydney, was taken over by Toronto interests. Ultimately, in 1910, the two were united under Toronto-Montreal ownership in the Dominion Steel Corporation. The Nova Scotia Steel and Coal Company, meanwhile, operated not only at its base in New Glasgow but also in coal and steel production at Sydney Mines. It was Nova Scotian-owned until 1917, when control was secured by New York investors. A further consolidation came in 1921, following the intervention of a group of British investors. Both Dominion and Scotia now became parts of the giant British Empire Steel Corporation (BESCO). Headquartered in Montreal, and with its board dominated throughout the 1920s by directors residing in Montreal, Toronto, London, or New York, BESCO enjoyed virtual monopoly control of the coal and steel industries in Nova Scotia.[12]

A further ingredient in the gathering conflict was the strong Cape Breton tradition of industrial trade unionism. Cape Breton miners had been organized since the establishment of the Provincial Workmen's Association on the island in 1881. After the turn of the century, the international unionism of the United Mine Workers of America began to gain adherents, and eventually in 1919 District 26 of that union was established as the representative unit of all Cape Breton miners. The strength of the union had deep cultural roots. Although ethnically diverse, the mining community was sufficiently dominated by Scottish and Catholic traditions that any division could be kept within manageable limits.[13] District 26 also had a strong and militant leadership, including its veteran secretary-treasurer J.B. McLachlan, who in the federal general election of 1921 succeeded in polling over 8,900 votes as a Labour candidate in Cape Breton South-Richmond.[14]

Labour-capital conflict was not new in the Maritimes in the 1920s. The years between the turn of the century and the First World War had seen increased union militancy at the same time as the ownership of industry was becoming increasingly concentrated, and a strike such as the 22-month Springhill miners' strike in 1909-11 was exceptional only in its length.[15] As recently as in 1919, a general strike in Amherst had pitted the Amherst Federation of Labour against major employers of the town, in the wake of layoffs at the Canadian Car and Foundry Company and protests against the higher wages and more regular work being offered to the company's Montreal employees. The results of the three-week strike were inconclusive, and in the years to come Amherst's economy was devastated by branch-plant closures. Nevertheless, the strike had been an early indication that the crisis following the First World War would be met forcefully by organized labour.[16]

In Cape Breton the most serious phase of the crisis began in early 1922, when BESCO announced a wage cut of 37.5 percent. Already workers in both coal and steel had been hard hit by plant closures and short-time working. The steel plant at Sydney Mines had closed for good in November 1920, while the larger plant in Sydney barely stayed open while reducing its output. Coal production, meanwhile, had also declined, and work was increasingly irregular. Whole communities were hard-pressed, so that even the shrewd management of the women who organized family finances — the miner's wife, McLachlan declared in January 1922, was "the greatest financier in the world" — was no longer adequate.[17] That the new wage reduction would be resisted was never in doubt, and the district convention of the U.M.W. in June 1922 went as far as to adopt radical resolutions calling for "the complete overthrow of the capitalist system and capitalist state."[18]

These "red declarations" brought expressions of concern from the international headquarters of the U.M.W., but were effectively endorsed by the District 26 membership in August, in the election of "Red Dan" Livingstone as district president and the re-election of McLachlan as secretary-treasurer. When the inevitable strike began on August 15th, the extent of the apprehension of some local officials became clear. On the request of a county court judge, some 500 regular troops converged on Cape Breton from Halifax and Quebec. One local Member of Parliament telegraphed Prime Minister Mackenzie King to ask for more. "People in terror of revolution which radical element threaten," the wire declared.[19] Within days a further 500 troops and 1000 special police were designated for Cape Breton. Suggestions that both Canadian and British warships should be ordered to Sydney harbour were seriously made, though not acted upon.

In the end the strike was largely non-violent. Eleven days after it had begun a settlement was reached. The pact was accepted, as Livingstone said, "under the muzzle of rifles, machine guns and gleaming bayonets," but for the time being the dispute was over.[20] The action of the miners had not succeeded in avoiding a wage cut, but it was to be 20 percent rather than the original 37.5 percent. The strike in itself — as opposed to the military reaction to it — had been undramatic, and certainly gave no indication of a revolution in the making. Yet the fears of company and government officials remained, and so too did the issues of wage reduction and shortage of work.

Conflict was resumed in the summer of 1923. This time the steelworkers went out on strike. Wages were at issue, as the Amalgamated Association of Iron, Steel and Tin Workers sought a 20 per cent increase to offset previous reductions. Even more important was the union's claim for management recognition, which had been withheld since the organization of the Sydney local in 1917. The strike began on 28 June, and two days later some 250 troops arrived on an armoured train. Two days after that the tension was heightened when special provincial police made an apparently unprovoked mounted charge through the Sydney district of Whitney Pier, causing a number of serious injuries. On 3 July, the miners voted to strike in support of the steelworkers; then on the 5th, McLachlan issued an open letter to all locals of District 26 condemning the police and the government of Nova Scotia for the Whitney Pier incident.[21] On the evening of the 6th, largely on the basis of this letter, McLachlan and Livingstone were arrested for seditious libel. Charges against Livingstone were later dropped, but McLachlan was convicted and served time in Dorchester Penitentiary during the early months of 1924.

McLachlan and Livingstone were also deposed as executive members of District 26, by the international union president. Yet the struggle continued. The 1923 strike continued until late July,

Steel strike, 1923

although failing to win concessions from the company. Towards the end of the year, BESCO announced a further 20 percent wage decrease for the miners, which was successfuly resisted in a strike in early 1924. The sequence of events was then repeated. The company renewed its demand in late 1924, and in March 1925 began a bitter five-month strike. Clashes between miners and company police led to a further intervention by the armed forces in June, some 2000 strong. Still violence continued, until the strike ended in August with the miners accepting wage cuts of between 6 and 8 percent.[22]

The settlement of 1925 was the final phase of the continuous confrontation which had lasted since early 1922. For the miners and steelworkers, it had been a rearguard action in the face of shrinking wages, but hardly a successful one. The defeat of 1923 effectively destroyed the steelworkers' union as it then existed, while the miners had to wait until the Second World War for their wage schedule to regain the level of 1920.[23] Nor did the company prosper. Rumoured from its beginnings in 1921 to be financially unstable, BESCO lurched towards bankruptcy in 1926 by defaulting on bond payments, and was finally dissolved in 1930 in favour of the new Dominion Steel and Coal Corporation. The epitaph of the socialist poet Dawn Fraser on the company was bitter: "may Satan's imps attend your hearse — adieu, adieu, Cape Breton's curse."[24]

BESCO had had a short and inglorious life. Historians are agreed that its labour practices sharpened class tensions, and the Duncan Royal Commission on Nova Scotia Coal Mining reported specifically in 1925 that its original demand for a 37.5 percent wage cut had been unjustified.[25] Nevertheless, in the end it was not the company which wore down the workers of Cape Breton, but the larger economic forces of industrial and regional decline. The cost was great. "The winter winds are bleak and drear," wrote Dawn Fraser during the hungry year of 1925, "methinks I better move from here."[26] Moving or staying, Cape Breton workers had already shown that they could form the cutting edge of resistance to economic pressures that threatened the entire fabric of Maritime society.

There was resistance also in the more formal settings of provincial and federal politics. In the immediate aftermath of the First World War, it had seemed that both political levels might be transformed by the intervention of new parties. Farmers' and labour movements sprang up throughout Canada and enjoyed varying degrees of success as pressure groups and political parties. In the Maritimes the province least affected was Prince Edward Island, where the industrial working class was small, while the concerns of farmers were so important that they were central to the policies of the existing political parties. The Island farmers' movement formed in early 1921, therefore, found itself confined for the most part to marginal issues in attempting to assert a distinctive identity.[27]

The New Brunswick experience was different, with the United Farmers fielding successful candidates in both federal and provincial elections. Their president, T.W. Caldwell, won a federal seat on behalf of the newly-formed Progressive party in the Victoria-Carleton by-election of November 1919, and in a provincial general election the following year, the farmers won six seats out of 48. The allied Labour party won two, to complete a respectable showing. In Nova Scotia, earlier in the year, farmers' and labour parties failed to arrive at an agreement to cooperate formally, but still seven farmers won seats in the 43-seat house, and four labour candidates, with a combined popular vote of 30.9 percent.[28]

Yet 1920 proved to be the high-water mark of farmer-labour success in the region. Caldwell narrowly gained re-election in the federal election of 1921, but no others joined him, in spite of McLachlan's substantial vote in Cape Breton. Instead, the great majority of Maritime seats — 25 out of 31 — went to the Liberal party of Mackenzie King, which ousted the existing Conservative government of Arthur Meighen in this election. Regional issues had dominated the campaign. Throughout 1920 the three Maritime provincial governments had coordinated representations to Ottawa on transportation and other issues, emphasizing the disastrous implications of rising freight rates. They had met with scant response, and one Conservative party statement went so far as to brand Maritime claims to lower freight rates as "rank sectionalism."[29] To such an attitude, the Progressive party could offer no satisfactory alternative, since most of its supporters in the west, who were much more numerous than in the Maritimes, favoured tariff and freight rates policies directly opposite to those that were in the Maritimes' best interests. The Liberals were the beneficiaries of the shortcomings of the other two parties.

Ironically, the election of 25 members of the governing party did not help to advance regional interests significantly. The King government was in a minority position, and depended for its survival on not offending the 64 Progressives, of whom the majority represented western constituencies. King, as Prime Minister, tended now to be more sympathetic to western than to Maritime interests, and yet of course continued to demand the party allegiance of the Maritime Liberal members.[30]

This impasse, again a consequence of the political decline of the Maritimes as a region within Confederation, could not readily be resolved within the existing Parliament. The years from 1922 to 1925 therefore saw the growth of an extra-parliamentary political movement for "Maritime Rights." The mood had also changed. While provincial governments and business interests had initially argued against freight rate alterations on the basis of the potential harm they could do, it was now clear that the time of warding off a future threat was gone. The damage was done, and the crisis was real.

The Maritime Rights movement was not monolithic. It drew support from boards of trade in towns and cities, from newspapers such as the Halifax *Herald* and the Saint John *Telegraph-Journal*, and from some provincial politicians, including the Liberal premier of New Brunswick, P.J. Veniot. Its goals ranged from general to specific. A general aim was to explain the Maritimes' grievances plainly to other Canadians. For that purpose, speakers were sent to centres throughout Canada, the leading exponent of the movement being H.S. Congdon, a Dartmouth journalist who proved adept at explaining why "it will not pay Canada to have these provinces destroyed . . . "[31] More specifically, leaders of the movement argued for revisions in freight rates, for use of Maritime ports rather than Portland, Maine, for shipping of Canadian goods, and for measures to stimulate immigration to the Maritime provinces, among other issues.

The climax of the initial phase of the Maritime Rights movement was reached in February 1925 when the Saint John board of trade sponsored a large delegation to Ottawa, intended to include a representative from every incorporated community in the region. Although that ideal was not reached, some 300 delegates did make the trip. Despite some confusion as to the exact arguments to be put to Prime Minister King on the morning of the 25th, the meeting was dominated by an effective and impassioned speech from the mayor of Saint John, John Murphy, who denounced the restrictions put upon the economic development of the region by federal policy. Mackenzie King was not impressed, and said so. His unwillingness to concede that the Maritimes had a case was consistent with the policy of the government since the election of 1921. In the new election of October 1925, the response of the voters was clear. The Conservatives won 23 seats, almost entirely reversing the Liberal tide of 1921. Whatever else the Maritime Rights movement may or may not have achieved, it had established its importance in regional electoral politics.[32]

The Maritime response to the conditions of the 1920s was not confined to the areas of politics and industrial relations. With industrial areas suffering from plant closures and slowdowns, and rural areas from decay and out-migration, the economic malaise of the region was a matter for general concern. As in the political arena, reform movements that immediately followed the First World War were transformed during the 1920s into instruments by which Maritimers put up what defence they could against economic pressures. Nowhere was this more true than in the area of higher education.

By 1920, higher education in the Maritime provinces was the responsibility of nine degree-granting colleges and universities, as well as professional training colleges and junior colleges. Many of the institutions were small, and the majority were associated with religious denominations. Most had no government funding, and had to be financed on the basis of tuition fees, church subsidies, and private donations. Increasingly in the early part of the twentieth century, they had turned to United States-based private foundations for assistance. The Carnegie Corporation of New York, one of the largest of these philanthropic organizations, decided in 1921 to commission a major study of higher education in the region, as a guide for future donations. The two commissioners, William S. Learned and Kenneth C.M. Sills, were senior academic administrators in the U.S., and in late 1921 they visited the Maritimes on an inspection tour.

Their recommendations, published in 1922, were potentially far-reaching. The most important was that six of the universities — Acadia, Dalhousie, King's, Mount Allison, the University of New Brunswick, and St. Francis Xavier — should join together in Halifax to form a federated University of the Maritime Provinces. By forming one large university to replace several small ones, the commissioners believed that higher academic quality would be achieved.[33] The scheme eventually failed to be realized, except that the University of King's College moved from its original site in Windsor, Nova Scotia, to a new location in Halifax, in close association with Dalhousie. With that exception, even the promise of a subsidy of $3 million from the Carnegie Corporation could not persuade the various institutions to comply.

More significant than the ultimate failure of the scheme, however, was the way in which it was discussed. From the beginning, the Carnegie commissioners had been aware that the decline of the Maritimes as a region within Confederation was a current political concern. Noting the Maritimes' "feeling of comparative poverty," they noted that "the adjustment of this inequality is now an issue in Canadian politics, or at least in that aspect of it that especially interests the Maritime Provinces."[34] This theme was taken up by the supporters of their proposals. "We talk about 'Maritime rights'," remarked President A.S. Mackenzie of Dalhousie, and yet "even the Western Universities, which are so much newer, have already gone way beyond us." James J. Tompkins, vice-president of St. Francis Xavier University, put the matter more bluntly by declaring that what was at issue was "justice for the Maritime Provinces in matters educational."[35]

Tompkins, in fact, took a different approach from Mackenzie and the more orthodox supporters of the federation scheme. Whereas they saw educational reform as contributing in a general way to alleviating regional problems, through providing highly-educated and professionally trained leadership at high levels of society, Tompkins saw education as a means by which communities could collectively take charge of their own destiny.

In 1921 he had established a "people's school" in Antigonish, aimed at offering instruction of university standard to participants such as farmers and "Labor leaders — actual and prospective," whose prior educational background was often limited to the early grades. Tompkins hoped that St. Francis Xavier would become "a people's college" within the proposed federation, and that a "Labour college" would also be included, based on the existing Workers' Educational Club in Glace Bay.[36]

Tompkins' views were not acceptable to the governing board of St. Francis Xavier, or to the Roman Catholic hierarchy that heavily influenced this Catholic university. In late 1922, he was relieved of his university duties and sent as parish priest to the small town of Canso. His removal was one serious blow to the chance of success for the university federation scheme. Another strong factor, however, was rural opposition to the centralization of the colleges in Halifax. Undoubtedly this opposition was partly influenced by conservative attitudes and by self-interest in small towns which did not want to lose a major local employer.

Yet there was more to it than that. From the beginning, critics of the federation scheme had argued that, at a time of acute rural crisis, it was absurd to centralize higher education and make students go to the expense of travelling long distances and living in a large city. Instead, undergraduate colleges should continue to offer education at modest cost in locations throughout the region. This view was strongly expounded in 1922 by Rev. Gregory McLellan of St. Dunstan's College in Prince Edward Island, who declared that the existing colleges had "opened their doors and made it possible for a great many young men and women to receive an Arts course," and that removal to Halifax would curtail these opportunities. Similar arguments were advanced in editorials in the student magazine of Acadia University, the *Acadia Athenaeum*, which pointed out that university consolidation would do nothing to solve the major rural evil of out-migration. More generally, President G.J. Trueman of Mount Allison defended the work of the small colleges in a newspaper article in 1926, suggesting that this style of undergraduate education would make it possible "not only [to] do our share in advancing human learning, but by thorough examination and development of our own resources, bring about such economic conditions as will enable this country [the Maritime provinces] to support an increasing and contented population."[37]

The refusal of the small-town colleges to move to Halifax was fatal to the Carnegie federation scheme, which was quietly allowed to lapse in 1929. What was clear, though, was that all participants in the debates regarded university reform as an issue inseparable from the regional need to respond to harsh economic conditions. Action also followed. Universities such as Acadia and Mount Allison expanded their facilities and their student numbers, though within self-imposed limits, so as to offer opportunities to students from a variety of social and geographical origins. St. Francis Xavier, despite the loss of Tompkins, continued to be active in adult education. Its extension department, formally inaugurated in 1928, would become famous as the originator of "Antigonish Movement" cooperatives in the 1930s. One observer from the United States — Morse Cartwright, director of the American Association for Adult Education — reflected in 1936 that the Maritime provinces and Newfoundland were "exceptional and quite unlike the situations that ordinarily would be met in the United States," in that "it seems quite impossible to separate the educational and the economic goals."[38] This comment revealed the extent to which the regional travails of the 1920s had changed the course of higher educational reform. Higher education had been mobilized in the interests of the larger struggle.

The larger struggle continued also in Ottawa. The 23 Conservative members of Parliament elected in the Maritimes in 1925 soon found themselves in the midst of a constitutional crisis. The 1925 election reduced the governing Liberals to only 99 seats out of 245. The 116 Conservatives could not claim a majority, however, and Prime Minister King attempted to soldier on with the acquiesence of the 24 Progressives. When this arrangement collapsed in June 1926, King asked the governor-general, Lord Byng, to call a new election. Byng refused. Instead, he called on Arthur Meighen's Conservatives to form a government. Only when Meighen also proved unable to command the confidence of the House of Commons was a general election called for September. This time Mackenzie King's Liberals, loudly proclaiming that the "King-Byng Affair" had been an example of a British governor-general thwarting the legitimate advice of a Canadian prime minister, were returned convincingly to power. Their 128 seats represented a clear majority.[39]

Two points arose from this episode which had especial significance for the Maritime provinces. First, that at a time when every vote was important, Mackenzie King finally recognized the political force of Maritime Rights advocacy. In early 1926, the King minority government announced the appointment of a federal royal commission to look into Maritime demands. Headed by the British lawyer Sir Andrew Rae Duncan, who had also headed the provincial royal commission on the Nova Scotia coal industry in the previous year, the commission began its hearings in July 1926.[40] The second point to emerge was that the Maritime electorate, however much the appointment of the Duncan commission may have been welcomed, was still in no mood to place its trust in the Liberal party. In the 1926 election the Liberals succeeded in winning back three New Brunswick seats, but still the Conservatives elected members in 20 of the 29 Maritime constituencies. The problem was, of course, that they would now sit in opposition rather than in government.[41]

The Duncan commission completed its report speedily. Although the full text did not appear until near the end of 1926, a preliminary version was delivered to Mackenzie King on 23 September, just over a week after his election victory. The report was forthright in conveying the Maritime provinces' sense of crisis and injustice. "It is not possible to exaggerate," declared one passage, "the dismay and depression with which some communities in Cape Breton look upon the approach of the winter season, in view of the distress arising through the irregularity of employment that is then experienced." In general, Duncan argued that a bright future was possible for the Maritime provinces, but with an important proviso: "if they are relieved of the disabilities under which they have been suffering and are enabled to approach their problems with renewed vigour." The commission had specific recommendations as to how this could be achieved. Its major proposals included a 20 per cent reduction in railway freight rates, increases in federal subsidies to the provincial governments so as to bring them into line with those paid to the central and western provinces, measures to promote port development in Halifax and Saint John, a subsidy to steel producers using locally-mined coal so as to compensate for lack of tariff protection, and upgrading of the Prince Edward Island ferry service.[42]

The Duncan report was described by the Halifax *Herald* as the "Magna Charta of the Maritimes."[43] However trite the phrase, there was no doubt that Duncan had made a serious effort to come to grips with the Maritime grievances. Had the report been implemented in an equally serious spirit, genuine change might have come about. By King and the cabinet, however, it was mined for politically expedient measures and then set aside. As summarized by E.R. Forbes, the historian of the Maritime Rights movement, "the cabinet . . . changed Duncan's program for

Halifax-Herald, page 1, Saturday, December 11, 1926

Maritime rehabilitation into a plan for Maritime pacification — a pacification to be achieved with the fewest possible concessions."[44] Of the major recommendations, the reduction in freight rates was implemented. So was the increase in provincial subsidies, but only on a temporary basis. National harbours boards were created for Halifax and Saint John, and incentives given for coking plants to use Canadian coal.

Many Maritime Rights leaders now declared that victory had been won. Only later did it become evident that those of Duncan's recommendations that had supposedly been deferred for further study had in fact been dropped entirely, and that even those implemented — such as the freight rate reduction — were to be subjected to narrow interpretations that would destroy much of their value.[45] For the moment the Maritime economy began in 1927 to experience an apparent revival. Pulp and paper markets were healthy, while the prosperity of other parts of North America led to significant growth in the tourist industry. Together with investment in new facilities at the major ports, these developments and related construction activity gave a temporary brightness to the economic picture. Yet the reality was that the Maritime provinces were left with no effective defence against the renewal of depression in 1929.

In the Maritime provinces, the 1920s comprised a decade of sustained though unsuccessful struggle against powerful economic forces. The struggle was one in which there were strong elements of regional solidarity, at times cutting across provincial, class, and ethnic boundaries. This is not to say that diversity and division did not exist. Class conflict in the Maritimes in the 1920s, for example, was not solely the result of tension between indigenous labour and outside capital, even though that was a major element. Instances of labour-capital dispute within regional society are not difficult to find, whether it be on the Minto coalfield in New Brunswick, where local ownership had persisted to a greater extent than on the larger Nova Scotia fields, or in the 1925 strike of women telephone operators in Halifax.[46]

Ethnic tensions and disparities are also easily documented in the Maritimes of the 1920s. Black and native communities continued to be economically and socially marginal. Despite the individual efforts of leaders such as the Baptist ministers James Kinney, Wellington Naey States, and William A. White, Black Maritimers were confronted with both overt and covert discrimination. The 1918 Nova Scotia Education Act, for example,

Logging Crew, Tupper Warren Pulp Sawmill, Weymouth Falls, N.S.

continued to provide for segregated schools, and shortage of funds and teachers ensured that during the 1920s Black children could rarely be certain of their education. At the same time, the rising unemployment levels led to erosion of already-limited opportunities for Black men and women. Some left for central Canada. Others fell back on the resources of family and community, where sharing and cooperation made economic survival possible.[47] The Micmac and Maliseet, meanwhile, were isolated on reserves. At a time when assimilation was the goal of the federal government, through the Department of Indian Affairs, it was not surprising that loss of native culture was a continuing process, though it was never complete.[48] Both Blacks and native people in the region would have to await the post-World War II years for the rebirth of their own struggles for due recognition.

The Acadian role in the region did change, meanwhile, at least in symbolic ways. Already by the opening of the 1920s, one major provincial political leader was an Acadian. Aubin-Edmond Arsenault had become the Conservative premier of Prince Edward Island in 1917, and remained as opposition leader for two years after his election defeat in 1919.[49] Arsenault's experience was then paralleled by that of Peter J. Veniot, who became premier of New

Brunswick in 1923, was defeated in 1925, and then went on to a career in federal politics by winning a seat in the 1926 federal election.[50] Yet real as these achievements were, they constituted only a phase in the Acadian struggle. It remained true that no Acadian had been *elected* to the premiership, even in New Brunswick where Acadians comprised one-third of the population. Both Arsenault and Veniot had been appointed to the office by their respective caucuses, following the resignations of their predecessors. Neither survived his first election in office. In the case of Veniot, the reasons for defeat were complex, including the effects of public frustration with the failure of the federal Liberal government to respond to regional concerns. Nevertheless, Veniot's race and religion did become a factor in the campaign. It was seriously alleged that the Ku Klux Klan, financed from New York, were actively involved. Although the statement of the provincial attorney-general that the Conservative leader's regalia consisted of "white hood and burning cross" was an exaggeration, there is no doubt that the premier's complaints of a whispering campaign against "Veniot the Frenchman" had some justification.[51] Not until the 1960s would New Brunswickers be ready to elect an Acadian premier.

Also reflected in the 1925 New Brunswick election was another kind of division within the Maritime region in the 1920s: on the question of social reform, especially as related to temperance and prohibition. Throughout most of the 1920s, all three Maritime provinces were officially "dry." Prohibition had extended throughout Prince Edward Island as early as 1906, was adopted in New Brunswick in 1917, and fully implemented in Nova Scotia in 1921 after several years during which the city of Halifax had been exempt. The prohibition movement, so often looked on with derision by later generations as an example of narrow-mindedness, had become in the late nineteenth century a genuine force for social reform, and a popular one. Such organizations as the Women's Christian Temperance Union had argued that alcohol abuse was not just a matter for individual shame, but was the root of many social problems and so deserved to be outlawed by legislation. A Canada-wide referendum in 1898 had resulted in majorities favouring prohibition in all three Maritime provinces.

Yet prohibition looked better in theory than in practice. Far from eliminating alcohol altogether, it led to flourishing trades in bootlegging within the region and export to the even more strictly prohibitionist United States. Prohibition was abandoned, in favour

Aubin-Edmond Arsenault

Peter J. Veniot

of government regulation of the liquor trade, in New Brunswick in 1927 and in Nova Scotia in 1929, though not in Prince Edward Island until 1948. While it lasted, it was a controversial issue, as Premier Veniot found out in 1925 when his government was accused by its electoral opponents of turning the liquor laws into a farce by non-enforcement. More generally, the abandonment of prohibition in two of the provinces signified erosion of the confidence of reformers within the churches and organizations such as the W.C.T.U., who a few years before had so firmly believed that the "social gospel" could bring about a transformation of society and its values.[52]

The prohibition issue was linked to other forms of division and disparity within the Maritimes in the 1920s. One was the question of gender. Women's organizations had played a major role in the prohibition movement, and there had been a close link with the campaign for votes for women. Women's suffrage was attained in Nova Scotia in 1918, in New Brunswick in 1919 — though in that province women could not run for office until 1934 — and in Prince Edward Island in 1922. In the Maritime provinces as elsewhere, however, the right to vote did not in itself remove the more subtle social and economic barriers to women's progress. Working-class women continued to be hired for low wages, while middle-class women enjoyed ready access only to professions — such as teaching, nursing, or other social service occupations — which were part of women's accepted sphere. Even within these limits, prospects were not necessarily good. Optimism, early in the decade, that social services would be permanently expanded as a consequence of the relief efforts that had followed the 1917 Halifax Explosion, was soon belied by harsh economic realities. Women in other occupations also faced hard struggles in attempting to fulfil their aspirations. For the Halifax telephone operators who struck against the Maritime Telephone Company in 1925 for higher wages, or for the Dalhousie University histologist Elizabeth Bean who was employed at the university in 1927 as a lab assistant to her less-qualified husband and never saw the quality of her 24 years service rewarded either in salary or in professorial rank, even the real achievements of the women's suffrage movement had left basic questions unsolved.[53]

If Maritimers were divided by class, ethnicity, and gender, as well as by questions of social reform, there also remained geographical disparities which reflected economic realities within the region. Rum-running to the United Sates was a lucrative business in many coastal areas of the Maritimes during the 1920s.

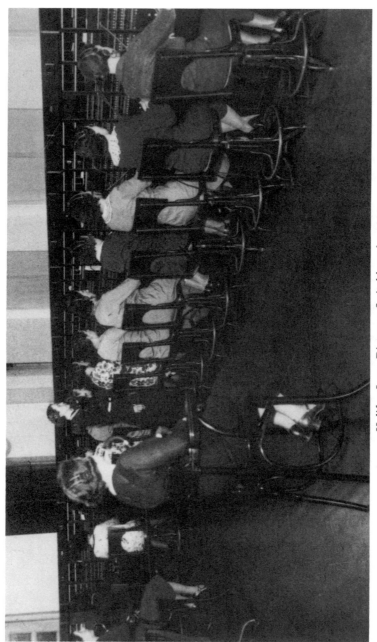

Halifax Long Distance Switchboard c.1930

So, on a more secure legal basis, was the fox-farming industry in Prince Edward Island. What these two disparate trades had in common, and in common with longer-established pillars of the regional economy such as lumber and fisheries, was that they depended on exports outside Canada. Rum-runners did not have to worry about trade barriers, because they operated outside the law. Other exporters naturally sought reduction of tariffs where possible, even to the point of advocating free trade arrangements with the United States. For the industrialized parts of the region which depended on selling in Canadian markets, however, tariff barriers were essential in order to keep out cheap foreign products. On this issue, even the Maritime Rights movement was unable to reach a united approach. The Duncan commission also avoided confronting directly the question of tariffs, though it noted the possibility of negotiating special trade treaties for commodities such as forest products and fish, while at the same time recording for the benefit of the government's Tariff Advisory Board the importance of protection to the coal and steel industries.[54] What the ambiguity most aptly revealed was the continuing difference in economic interests between industrialized and non-industrialized areas.

For all these reasons, it would be misleading to portray the Maritime provinces as being united or homogeneous in the 1920s. A long history of ethnic and social diversity, along with the effects of nineteenth-century industrialization, had created a complex society. Nevertheless, in one sense it is possible to identify a commonality of experience during this crucial decade. The pressures of economic disaster were virtually universally felt. Obviously they were not felt in the same ways by people of different social backgrounds or geographical locations, and yet the struggle to cope with harsh economic realities was the struggle of all. So was the effort to resist, using whatever means might be available.

In that effort, divisions could be transcended. Reconciliation of religious and ethnic differences among Cape Breton miners, for example, was strongly and successfully advocated by union leaders.[55] The setting aside of class differences was characteristic of the early years of the Maritime Rights movement when, for example, the Railway Brotherhoods joined with business interests in attacking cutbacks imposed in the region by the newly-established Canadian National Railways.[56] Deep philosophical differences might also be suspended, as when the radical but non-Marxist James Tompkins corresponded cordially in 1922 with the

Marxist J.B. McLachlan on the possible Labour College within the projected university federation.[57] The prominence of economic and social issues in that entire debate over the educational issue of university reform was in itself evidence of the pervasive importance of the economic crisis. More generally, so too was the way in which the electorate — newly expanded to encompass universal adult suffrage — voted so clearly in election after election on the basis of which party seemed best able to advance the regional cause.

These elements of unified action, within a society which contained all the disparities and contradictions that its complex past had bequeathed, demonstrated the exceptional character of the 1920s as a decade in Maritime history. For reasons that were partly international in scope, but also partly Canadian-made, the Maritime provinces met an economic crisis of unprecedented severity. That resistance to it was largely unsuccessful was not surprising, but was nonetheless of crucial importance for later generations who would face the choice of either living elsewhere altogether or living in a region of Canada suffering from deep-seated economic problems. That resistance was strong, however, is a point that has all too often been overlooked by those who believe in the stereotype of the quaint but quiescent Maritime provinces. The 1920s was a decade of struggle. If nothing else, the national attention gained by the capital-labour disputes in Cape Breton and by the Maritime Rights movement showed that regional disparity could be — perhaps even should be — regarded as a Canadian rather than a local problem. It was ultimately a decade in which important elements of the provinces' economic well-being were surrendered; but at least they were not surrendered easily.

NOTES

1. Frank H. Underhill, *The Image of Confederation* (Toronto, 1964), p. 63.
2. Saunders, *Economic History*, pp. 37-42.
3. T.W. Acheson, "The Maritimes and 'Empire Canada'," in Bercuson, *Canada and the Burden of Unity*, p. 95.
4. L.D. McCann, "Metropolitanism and Branch Businesses in the Maritimes, 1881-1931," *Acadiensis*, 13 (Autumn 1983), pp. 112-13.
5. McCann, "The Mercantile-Industrial Transition in the Metal Towns of Pictou County," pp. 50-61; K. Inwood, "A Merger Bid Which Failed: the 1910 Raid on Scotia," paper presented to Canadian Historical Association Annual Meeting, Winnipeg, 1986, pp. 13-17.
6. F.H. Leacy, ed., *Historical Statistics of Canada* (2nd ed.; Ottawa, 1983), series A2-14.
7. Ernest R. Forbes, *The Maritime Rights Movement, 1919-1927: A Study in Canadian Regionalism* (Montreal, 1979), pp. 13-17.
8. Forbes, *Aspects of Maritime Regionalism*, p. 13; David Frank, "The Cape Breton Coal Industry and the Rise and Fall of the British Empire Steel Corporation," *Acadiensis*, 7 (Autumn 1977), p. 9.
9. Forbes, "Misguided Symmetry," p. 70; Cruikshank, "The People's Railway," pp. 92-4, 98-100.
10. Forbes, *Aspects of Maritime Regionalism*, p. 18.
11. Saunders, *Economic History*, pp. 42, 64-5; *Report of the Royal Commission Investigating the Fisheries of the Maritime Provinces and the Magdalen Islands* (Ottawa, 1928), p. 9; Andrew Hill Clark, *Three Centuries and the Island: A Historical Geography of Settlement and Agriculture in Prince Edward Island, Canada* (Toronto, 1959), pp. 121, 128, 150, 172; Gene Barrett, "Capitalism and the Fisheries of Atlantic Canada to 1940" (unpublished manuscript), pp. 35-40; Kennedy Wells, *The Fishery of Prince Edward Island* (Charlottetown, 1986), pp. 159-60.
12. Frank, "The Cape Breton Coal Industry and the Rise and Fall of the British Empire Steel Corporation," pp. 8-23.
13. David Frank, "Tradition and Culture in the Cape Breton Mining

Community in the Early Twentieth Century," in Kenneth Donovan, ed., *Cape Breton at 200: Historical Essays in Honour of the Island's Bicentennial, 1785-1985* (Sydney, 1985), pp. 203-18.

14. David Frank and Nolan Reilly, "The Emergence of the Socialist Movement in the Maritimes, 1899-1916," in Robert J. Brym and R. James Sacouman, eds., *Underdevelopment and Social Movements in Atlantic Canada* (Toronto, 1979), p. 101; Anthony MacKenzie, "The Rise and Fall of the Farmer-Labor Party in Nova Scotia" (M.A. thesis; Dalhousie University, 1969), pp. 137-49.
15. Ian McKay, "Strikes in the Maritimes, 1901-1914," *Acadiensis*, 13 (Autumn 1983), pp. 3-46.
16. Nolan Reilly, "The General Strike in Amherst, Nova Scotia, 1919," *Acadiensis*, 9 (Spring 1980), pp. 56-77.
17. *Sydney Post*, 21 January 1922, quoted in David Frank, "The Miner's Financier: Women in the Cape Breton Coal Towns, 1917," *Atlantis*, 8 (Spring 1983), p. 137.
18. Quoted in David Frank, "The Trial of J.B. McLachlan," *Historical Papers: Vancouver 1983*, p. 209.
19. Quoted in Don Macgillivray, "Military Aid to the Civil Power: The Cape Breton Experience in the 1920s," *Acadiensis*, 3 (Spring 1974), pp. 50-1.
20. *Maritime Labour Herald*, 23 June 1923, quoted in *ibid.*, p. 54.
21. Macgillivray, "Military Aid to the Civil Power," p. 56; Frank, "The Trial of J.B. McLachlan," pp. 212-13.
22. Macgillivray, "Military Aid to the Civil Power," pp. 62-3; Paul MacEwan, *Miners and Steelworkers: Labour in Cape Breton* (Toronto, 1976), p. 146.
23. Macgillivray, "Military Aid to the Civil Power," p. 64.
24. Dawn Fraser, *Echoes from Labor's War: Industrial Cape Breton in the 1920s*, with introduction by David Frank and Donald Macgillivray (Toronto, 1976), pp. 84-5.
25. Forbes, *Maritime Rights*, p. 59.
26. Fraser, *Echoes from Labor's War*, p. 82.
27. Forbes, *Maritime Rights*, p. 45.
28. *Ibid.*, p. 47; Arthur T. Doyle, *Front Benches and Back Rooms: A Story of Corruption, Muckraking, Raw Partisanship and Intrigue in New Brunswick* (Toronto, 1976), pp. 212-16; MacKenzie, "Rise and Fall of the Farmer-Labor Party," passim.
29. Quoted in Forbes, *Maritime Rights*, p. 80.
30. Forbes, *Maritime Rights*, p. 87; John Herd Thompson with Allen Seager, *Canada, 1922-1939: Decades of Discord* (Toronto, 1985), pp. 14-17.
31. H.S. Congdon to J.V. Mackenzie, 31 October 1923, quoted in Forbes, *Maritime Rights*, p. 107.
32. Forbes, *Maritime Rights*, chapters vi, vii.
33. William S. Learned and Kenneth C.M. Sills, *Education in the Maritime Provinces of Canada* (New York, 1922), passim.

34. *Ibid.*, p. 5.
35. A.S. Mackenzie to G.J. Trueman, 30 April 1926, Dalhousie University Archives, DAL/MS/1/3. J.J. Tompkins to W.S. Learned, 2 April 1922, Carnegie Corporation Archives, Maritime Provinces Educational Federation Files; cited by permission of the Carnegie Corporation of New York.
36. J.J. Tompkins to F.J. Ney, 11 April 1921, J.J. Tompkins Papers, Beaton Institute, Sydney, N.S., MG10-2, 5(a); see also John G. Reid, "Health, Education, Economy: Philanthropic Foundations in the Atlantic Region in the 1920s and 1930s," *Acadiensis*, 14 (Autumn 1984), p. 74.
37. *Minutes of a Conference of Representatives of Maritime Provinces Universities and Colleges* (Halifax, 1922), p. 58; *Acadia Athenaeum*, Vol. 48, No. 6, May 1922, p. 72, and Vol. 49, No. 4, March 1923, p. 43; *Morning Chronicle* (Halifax), 28 January 1926.
38. Morse A. Cartwright to F.P. Keppel, 24 April 1936, Carnegie Corporation Archives, St. Dunstan's College File.
39. Thompson and Seager, *Canada, 1922-1939*, pp. 114-27, 334-5.
40. Forbes, *Maritime Rights*, p. 149.
41. Thompson and Seager, *Canada, 1922-1939*, pp. 124-8, 335.
42. *Report of the Royal Commission on Maritime Claims* (Ottawa, 1926), pp. 36, 44, and passim.
43. *Halifax Herald*, 11 December 1926.
44. Forbes, *Maritime Rights*, p. 176.
45. *Ibid.*, pp. 182-91.
46. Allan Seager, "Minto, New Brunswick: A Study in Canadian Class Relations Between the Wars," *Labour/Le Travailleur*, 5 (1980), p. 93; Bryan D. Palmer, *Working-Class Experience: The Rise and Reconstitution of Canadian Labour, 1800-1980* (Toronto, 1983), p. 197.
47. Robin W. Winks, *The Blacks in Canada: A History* (Montreal, 1971), pp. 325-6, 348-50, 379-80; G.A. Rawlyk, "The Guysborough Negroes: A Study in Isolation," *Dalhousie Review*, 48 (1968-9), p. 35; James W. St. G. Walker, "Black History in the Maritimes: Major Themes and Teaching Strategies," in Buckner, *Teaching Maritime Studies*, p. 100.
48. Wilson D. Wallis and Ruth Sawtell Wallis, "Culture Loss and Culture Change among the Micmac of the Canadian Maritime Provinces, 1912-1950," in H.F. McGee, Jr., *The Native Peoples of Atlantic Canada: A History of Indian-European Relations* (Ottawa, 1983), pp. 120-51.
49. J.-Henri Blanchard, *The Acadians of Prince Edward Island, 1720-1964* ([Charlottetown], 1964), pp. 99-100.
50. Philippe Doucet, "Politics and the Acadians," in Daigle, *The Acadians of the Maritimes*, p. 256.
51. Doyle, *Front Benches and Back Rooms*, pp. 254-8; on the operations of the Ku Klux Klan in New Brunswick, see also B.J. Grant, *When Rum was King: The Story of the Prohibition Era in New Brunswick* (Fredericton, 1984), pp. 40-5.
52. See E.R. Forbes, "Prohibition and the Social Gospel in Nova Scotia," *Acadiensis*, 1 (Autumn 1971), pp. 11-36.

53. Veronica Strong-Boag, "The Girl of the New Day: Canadian Working Women in the 1920s," *Labour/Le Travailleur*, 4 (1979), p. 155; Judith Fingard, "Gender and Inequality at Dalhousie: Faculty Women Before 1950," *Dalhousie Review*, 64 (1984-85), pp. 693-5. See also Conrad, *Recording Angels*, p. 24; Tulloch, *We, the Undersigned*, pp. 61-3, 107.
54. *Report of the Royal Commission on Maritime Claims*, pp. 34-7.
55. Frank, "Tradition and Culture in the Cape Breton Mining Community," p. 207.
56. E.R. Forbes, "The Origins of the Maritime Rights Movement," *Acadiensis*, 15 (Autumn 1975), pp. 59-60.
57. Reid, "Health, Education, Economy," p. 74.

FURTHER
READING

As a decade in Maritime history the 1920s have recently attracted
a great deal of attention. Much of the most important writing is found
in historical journals, although there are also a number of relevant books.
For general background in Canadian history, good starting-points are
Robert Craig Brown and Ramsay Cook, *Canada, 1896-1921: A Nation
Transformed* (McClelland and Stewart, Toronto, 1974), and John Herd
Thompson with Allen Seager, *Canada, 1922-1939: Decades of Discord*
(McClelland and Stewart, Toronto, 1985). On the history of the region
itself, Ernest R. Forbes, *The Maritime Rights Movement, 1919-1927: A Study
in Canadian Regionalism* (McGill-Queen's University Press, Montreal, 1979)
provides an excellent introduction as well as a specific treatment of the
Maritime Rights movement. The same author's shorter *Aspects of Maritime
Regionalism, 1867-1927* (Canadian Historical Association, Ottawa, 1983)
places the 1920s in a longer-term context.

On the economic issues that were so central to Maritime history in
the 1920s, no one authoritative account exists. Useful perspectives dating
from the inter-war years themselves include the *Report of the [Duncan]
Royal Commission on Maritime Claims* (Ottawa, 1926), and S.A. Saunders,
The Economic History of the Maritime Provinces (2nd edition, ed. T.W.
Acheson; Acadiensis Press, Fredericton, 1984). Important recent
discussions include the following: T.W. Acheson, "The Maritimes and
'Empire Canada'," in David Jay Bercuson, ed., *Canada and the Burden of
Unity* (Macmillan, Toronto, 1977), pp. 87-114; David Alexander, "Economic
Growth in the Atlantic Region, 1880-1940," *Acadiensis*, 8 (Autumn 1978),
pp. 47-76; Ken Cruikshank, "The People's Railway: The Intercolonial
Railway and the Canadian Public Enterprise Experience," *Acadiensis*, 16
(Autumn 1986), pp. 78-100; Ernest R. Forbes, "Misguided Symmetry: The
Destruction of Regional Transportation Policy for the Maritimes," in
Bercuson, *Canada and the Burden of Unity*, pp. 60-86; David Frank, "The
Cape Breton Coal Industry and the Rise and Fall of the British Empire
Steel Corporation," *Acadiensis*, 7 (Autumn 1977), pp. 3-34; L.D. McCann,

"The Mercantile-Industrial Transition in the Metal Towns of Pictou County, 1857-1931," *Acadiensis* 10 (Spring 1981), pp. 29-64; McCann, "Metropolitanism and Branch Businesses in the Maritimes, 1881-1931," *Acadiensis,* 13 (Autumn 1983), pp. 112-25. These articles tend to concentrate on the more industrialized parts of the region; for a discussion of the less industrialized Acadian economy, see Aurèle Young, "The Acadian Economy, History and Development," in Jean Daigle, ed., *The Acadians of the Maritimes: Thematic Studies* (Centre d'études acadiennes, Moncton, 1982), pp. 197-218. The economy of Prince Edward Island is treated in Lorne C. Callbeck, "Economic and Social Development Since Confederation," in F.W.P. Bolger, ed., *Canada's Smallest Province: A History of P.E.I.* (P.E.I. Centennial Commission, Charlottetown, 1973), pp. 328-54; Frank Schwartz, "An Economic History of Prince Edward Island," in Harry Baglole, ed., *Exploring Island History: A Guide to the Historical Resources of Prince Edward Island* (Belfast, P.E.I., 1977), pp. 93-116; and Kennedy Wells, *The Fishery of Prince Edward Island* (Ragweed Press, Charlottetown, 1986).

The labour and working-class history of the 1920s has been well treated by a number of recent authors. Studies by David Frank include "The Cape Breton Coal Miners, 1917-1926" (Ph.D. thesis; Dalhousie University, 1979); "Class Conflict in the Coal Industry: Cape Breton 1922," in Gregory S. Kealey and Peter Warrian, eds., *Essays in Canadian Working Class History* (McClelland and Stewart, Toronto, 1976) pp. 161-84; "The Miner's Financier: Women in the Cape Breton Coal Towns, 1917," *Atlantis,* 8 (Spring 1983), pp. 137-43; "The Trial of J.B. McLachlan," *Historical Papers: Vancouver 1983,* pp. 208-25; and "Tradition and Culture in the Cape Breton Mining Community in the Early Twentieth Century," in Kenneth Donovan, ed., *Cape Breton at 200: Historical Essays in Honour of the Island's Bicentennial, 1785-1985* (University College of Cape Breton Press, Sydney, 1985), pp. 203-18. Nolan Reilly has explored the Amherst experience in "The General Strike in Amherst, Nova Scotia, 1919," *Acadiensis,* 9 (Spring 1980) pp. 56-77, and Allen Seager that of Minto in "Minto, New Brunswick: A Study of Class Relations Between the Wars," *Labour/Le Travailleur,* 5 (1980), pp. 81-132. On the labour movement as an electoral force, see Anthony MacKenzie, "The Rise and Fall of the Farmer-Labor Party in Nova Scotia" (M.A. thesis; Dalhousie University, 1969). An important aspect of the Cape Breton conflicts is discussed in Don Macgillivray, "Military Aid to the Civil Power: The Cape Breton Experience in the 1920s," *Acadiensis,* 3 (Spring 1974), pp. 45-64, while he and Frank provide the introduction to Dawn Fraser's poems in *Echoes from Labour's War: Industrial Cape Breton in the 1920s* (New Hogtown Press, Toronto, 1976). Book-length treatments of aspects of the Cape Breton experience can be found in Paul MacEwan, *Miners and Steelworkers: Labour in Cape Breton* (Hakkert, Toronto, 1976), and John Mellor, *The Company Store: James Bryson McLachlan and the Cape Breton Coal Miners, 1900-1925* (Doubleday, Toronto, 1983), while a useful general perspective is offered by Bryan D. Palmer, *Working-Class Experience: The Rise and*

Reconstitution of Canadian Labour, 1800-1980 (Butterworth, Toronto, 1983).

Other social and political reform movements have also attracted the attention of historians. Forbes's *The Maritime Rights Movement* is one important work, as is the collection of essays edited by Robert J. Brym and R. James Sacouman, *Underdevelopment and Social Movements in Atlantic Canada* (New Hogtown Press, Toronto, 1979). Some aspects of educational reform are discussed in John G. Reid, *Mount Allison University: A History, to 1963*, Volume II (UTP, Toronto, 1984). Treatments of the social gospel, the temperance movement, and the results of prohibition, include C. Mark Davis, "Atlantic Canada's Rum Running Tradition," *Acadiensis*, 14 (Spring 1985), pp. 147-56; Ernest R. Forbes, "Prohibition and the Social Gospel in Nova Scotia," *Acadiensis*, 1 (Autumn 1971), pp. 11-36; B.J. Grant, *When Rum was King: The Story of the Prohibition Era in New Brunswick* (Fiddlehead Books, Fredericton, 1984); and Clifford Rose, *Four Years With the Demon Rum, 1925-1929*, ed. E.R. Forbes and A.A. MacKenzie (Acadiensis Press, Fredericton, 1980). Useful discussion of the political dimensions of reform can be found in Arthur J. Doyle, *Front Benches and Back Rooms: A Story of Corruption, Muck-Raking, Raw Partisanship and Intrigue in New Brunswick* (Green Tree Publishing, Toronto, 1976), and G.A. Rawlyk, "The Farmer-Labour Movement and the Failure of Socialism in Nova Scotia," in Laurier La Pierre et al., eds., *Essays on the Left: Essays in Honour of T.C. Douglas* (McClelland and Stewart, Toronto, 1971), pp. 31-41.

The role of women and the women's movement in the Maritimes in the 1920s has yet to be comprehensively studied. Discussion of certain important aspects can be found in Veronica Strong-Boag, "The Girl of the New Day: Canadian Working Women in the 1920s," *Labour/Le Travailleur*, 4 (1979), pp. 131-64; Judith Fingard, "Gender and Inequality at Dalhousie," *Dalhousie Review*, 64 (1984-5), pp. 687-703; Elspeth Tulloch, *We, the Undersigned: A Historical Overview of New Brunswick Women's Political and Legal Status, 1786-1984* (New Brunswick Advisory Council on the Status of Women, Moncton, 1985); and Linda Kealey, ed., *A Not Unreasonable Claim: Women and Reform in Canada, 1880s-1920s* (Women's Educational Press, Toronto, 1979). On the Black and Indian experience of the decade, see Robin W. Winks, *The Blacks in Canada: A History* (McGill-Queen's University Press, Montreal, 1971), and H.F. McGee, Jr., *The Native Peoples of Atlantic Canada: A History of Indian-European Relations* (Carleton University Press, Ottawa, 1983). The Acadian role has been more extensively studied, a good starting point being the essays in Daigle, ed., *The Acadians of the Maritimes: Thematic Studies*. For stimulating essays on all these topics, and others in the interdisciplinary field of Maritime Studies, see also P.A. Buckner, ed., *Teaching Maritime Studies* (Acadiensis Press, Fredericton, 1986).

EPILOGUE

In the writing of Maritime history, myths have abounded. There is the myth that the French were capable of colonizing Acadia simply through their own efforts, rather than on the sufferance of native people. There is the myth that the Acadian deportation was the result of one individual's personal villainy, whether Charles Lawrence or Jean-Louis Le Loutre. There is the myth that the Loyalists were idealists who effortlessly spread their benevolent influence far and wide. There is the myth that Confederation was purely a political question. There is the myth that the Maritime economy suddenly collapsed after reaching the height of its "Golden Age." And there is the myth that the economic burdens, which the region certainly did have to carry from the 1920s on, were passively and docilely accepted. These mythologies had varying origins. Some represented the conscious efforts of later generations to come to terms with aspects of their past. Some were the unconscious products of biased assumptions. Some were simply the best interpretations that could be made on the basis of sketchy available evidence. What all have in common is that they are too simplistic to do justice to the complex realities of past eras.

Not that any historian, even today, has a right to be complacent. Every generation re-interprets its past, and there is no doubt that very few years will have to go by before the historians of the 1980s will be rebuked for shortcomings of analysis and for the new mythologies that may have resulted. Nevertheless, recent years have seen a major effort by historians to reshape the way in which the Maritimes' past is perceived, in effect to reclaim the history of the region from long years of neglect. The same can be said of scholars of other groups whose past was long ignored in Canadian history — native people, Blacks, Acadians, women, the working class — and it is significant that all of these have importance in the new Maritime history. The result is a view of the past that not only allows for social complexity, but in fact puts struggle and diversity at the heart of historical interpretation.

The reality is that the historical evolution of the Maritime provinces has indeed been complex. While the study of selected decades cannot do full justice to all important developments, it can provide an introduction to the scope of the changes that have taken place. The issues were already complex in the 1600s when the Micmac redirected the course of the region's human history — for better or worse — by allowing French colonization to begin. A futher change in direction took place in the 1750s, when a dubious military interpretation of the nature of Acadian loyalties led to the forced removal of most of the non-native population from the region. The Acadians were soon replaced by new settlers on their lands, but it was in the 1780s when a further wave of migrations resulted in radical rearrangement of settlement patterns and the redrawing of the political map. By this time, the Maritime colonies had a population characterized by ethnic variety, and continuing immigration by Scots, Irish, and others would add to the diversity of identities and experiences among the peoples of the region.

It was this varied society that faced the Confederation debates of the 1860s. Entry into the Dominion of Canada had obvious political implications. It also had economic implications. What was clear to all was that the regional economy would soon be transformed by the influence of new technologies, and the Confederation option meant committing the Maritime provinces to a development strategy based on railway linkage to central Canada. The 1880s saw this strategy bear fruit, with the stimulus of the National Policy. Like all the others, however, this was a complex as well as a crucial decade: significant questions were raised as to how far the 1880s industrialization provided a sound basis for lasting economic health. At the same time, there was no going back. By the 1920s, a combination of economic and political factors had made all too real the fears that some had expressed forty years before. Against a background of worldwide economic disruption, control of major Maritime industries was now in the hands of outside capital, and the political decline of the Maritimes within Canada impeded effective defence of regional interests. The result was an economic collapse, although not without stiff resistance by Maritimers in arenas ranging from Cape Breton pitheads to Ottawa committee rooms.

The bitter experience of the 1920s illustrated a recurring theme of Maritime history: that for many of the people who lived in the region and participated in the major turning-points, the personal stakes were very high. For Indian people confronted by disease and culture change, for deported Acadians, for Black Loyalists thrust to the fringes of society, for rural Maritimers caught in declining communities in the late nineteenth and early twentieth centuries, for Cape Breton miners of the 1920s, happy endings were the exception rather than the rule. Nevertheless, another recurring theme lies in the tenacity with which adversity was met. Although ordinary people in the Maritimes have often been buffeted by strong political, military, and economic forces, self-direction has never been lightly surrendered.

In many ways the economic problems bequeathed by the 1920s have yet to be solved. Despite the general increase in Canadian standards of living since the Second World War, the Maritime provinces continue to suffer from high unemployment and relatively low average incomes. The characteristic solution of the 1960s and 1970s — federal subsidies, along with development of service industries — has brought about no dramatic change. A new solution will not be found simply by studying the history of the region, for history teaches no direct lessons of that kind. What the accurate study of history can do, however, is to save later generations from being the prisoners of past mythologies. In that sense, a revised view of the past is the first prerequisite for an unblinkered approach to the present and the future.

INDEX

Collège Ste-Joseph, 141-2;
Confederation, 93, 102-18, 129-31, 135-8,
    150-1, 163, 193, 194;
Congdon, H.S., 172;
Conservative party, 108, 129, 136, 138,
    171-2, 175-6, 179;
Cornwallis, Edward, 36, 48;
Corte-Real Gaspar, 10;
Cumberland County, N.S., 75, 111, 118,
    132;
Cuyler, Abraham, 68

Dalhousie University, 173, 182;
Dartmouth, 37, 172;
D'Aulnay, Charles de Menou, 29;
Deindustrialization, 165, 172, 194;
Delaware, 65;
De Monts, Pierre du Gua, 4-13, 14, 15, 19,
    21, 22;
DesBarres, Joseph Frederick Wallet, 68;
Digby, 75;
Dochet's Island. *See* St. Croix Island;
Drummond, Robert, 148;
Duncan, Sir Andrew Rae, 170, 176-8, 184;
Durham, John George Lambton, Earl of, 93,
    104

Economic development, 96, 98, 113-18,
    127-31, 136, 178;
Eddy, Jonathan, 62;
Education, 32, 83, 141-3, 172-5, 178-9, 182,
    185;
Elections, 76, 82, 110-11, 129, 138, 167,
    170-2, 175-6, 179-80, 185;
English, 94;
Expulsion, Acadian, 41-51, 79

Fenians, 110;
Fielding, William Stevens, 137-8, 148;
First World War, 161-4, 167, 170;
Fisheries, 3, 10-11, 16, 41, 42, 48, 72, 96,
    117, 130-1, 132, 137, 150, 162, 165,
    184;
Fitzgerald, Gerald, 77;
Flesché, Jessé, 14-15, 19;
Foreign Protestants, 36-7, 48, 49, 51, 94
Fort Beauséjour, 34, 38-41, 42, 43, 62;
Fort Gaspereau, 40;
Fort Lawrence, 34;
France, 4-17, 21-2, 29-32, 37-41, 42, 46, 48,
    51, 61, 63;
Fraser, Dawn, 170;
Fraser, James A., 151;
Fredericton, 78, 79, 83, 94, 96, 130, 143;
Freight rates, 164, 166, 171, 176, 178;

Frontenac, Louis de Buade, Comte de, 30;
Fundy, Bay of, 8, 18, 21, 34, 37, 47, 96, 98;
Fur trade, 3-4, 9-11, 14-16, 18, 20, 30

Georgetown, 117;
Georgia, 46;
Glace Bay, 174;
Gladstone, William Ewart, 102, 109;
Golden Age, 93, 97, 127-8, 151, 193;
Gordon, Arthur Hamilton, 109-10;
Grand Pré, 33, 43, 46, 139;
Gray, John Hamilton, 108;
Great Britain, 29-32, 36, 37-41, 42, 46, 48,
    51, 61, 63-4, 93, 96, 97, 100, 101-3,
    105, 109-12, 132, 135, 136, 144;
Guercheville, Antoinette de Pons, Marquise
    de, 16-17;
Guy, John, 12-13;
Guysborough, 83;
Guysborough County, N.S., 74, 75, 97

Halifax, 33, 36-7, 43, 48, 49, 50, 51, 63, 66,
    70, 74, 75-7, 96, 100, 130, 164, 168,
    173-4, 176, 178, 180, 182;
Hardy, Elias, 82;
Henry IV, King of France, 4, 8, 9, 11, 15;
Hopson, Peregrine Thomas, 38, 42, 48;
Howatt, Cornelius, 108;
Howe, Joseph, 110-12, 118

Ile Madame, 68;
Ile Royale. *See* Cape Breton Island;
Ile Saint-Jean. *See* Prince Edward Island;
Immigration, 29, 32, 36-7, 49-50, 61, 65-84,
    93-4, 172, 194;
Indian Island, 78, 110;
Industrialization, 98, 113-17, 128-31, 132,
    134-5, 138, 143-6, 148, 150-1, 161,
    184, 194;
Intercolonial Railway, 100-3, 113-16, 129,
    135, 164;
Irish, 29, 77, 94, 97, 110, 194;
Island of St. John. *See* Prince Edward
    Island

Jesuits, 16-17, 19

Kennebecasis Balley, 79;
Killam, Thomas, 117;
King, William Lyon Mackenzie, 168,
    171, 172, 175-6;
Kingsclear, 78;
King's College. Fredericton, *See*
    University of New Brunswick
King's College, Windsor, 83, 173;

PHOTO CREDITS